I HAD NO MONEY AND I LIKED IT

THE ABUNDANT JOURNEY OF AN OPEN HEART

LILOU MACE

Published by Juicy Living Publishing 2011

First published in 2011 by Juicy Living Publishing.

www.LilouMace.com
www.JuicyLivingPublishing.com

ISBN: 978-0-9562546-6-5

This book is dedicated to all my beautiful co-creators around the world.

REVIEWS

"It is impossible to open Lilou Mace's second book *I Had No Money and I Liked It* without experiencing a jolt of life-shifting possibility. This is a manifesto of sorts, full of hope and wisdom, from a writer who delights in life and leads by example."

- Barnet Bain, Producer, *What Dreams May Come*

"*I Had No Money and I Liked It* is a peek inside the daily life of a master manifestor. Lilou is deliberate in applying Law of Attraction to her daily life, and this book uncovers the unfolding and manifestation of events in her delicious life. I call this book, Life Lessons with Lilou. Get inspired with I Had No Money and I Liked."

- Michael Losier, author of *Law of Attraction* and *Law of Connection*

"Lilou Mace demonstrates the truth by leaping from the known into the unknown. As she finds challenges along the way, Lilou realizes that there is no other way to grow unless she faces her limitations. When she overcomes, Lilou opens her heart and finds the universe always responds. Be inspired by one's journey through the labyrinth of life."

- Dr Joe Dispenza, author of *Evolve Your Brain: The Science of Changing Your Mind* and *Breaking the Habit of Being Yourself: How to Lose Your Mind and Create a New One*. Also featured in the multi-award winning film, *What the Bleep Do We Know?*

"At a time when so many are fixated on money, Lilou has redefined "assets & resources" in terms of the fullness she feels in her heart from all the love she infuses into the world. We can all learn a lesson from her."

- Dr. Jacob Liberman, author of *Light: Medicine of The Future, Take off Your Glasses and See*, and *Wisdom From an Empty Mind*

"Lilou took the leap so many people wish they could take. Facing adversity she turned to her heart to guide her – what her heart told her seemed absurd, but she followed it. This is an inspirational, TRUE, story of one woman's courage to go with her gut. Along the way, Lilou found her gifts and her truly special path - this book is a gift to all who seek to find their own unique way in the world."

- Freeman Michaels, radio show host and author of *Weight Release: A Liberating Journey*

"Whatever you can do, or dream you can, begin it. Boldness has genius, power and magic in it." Lilou lives this powerful message. I have witnessed her genius, as she was the driving force in getting www.CoCreatingOurReality.com into the world, and again with her books and The Juicy Living Tour. Her inspiration continues to impact millions of people around the world! It is a joy to watch Lilou...Lilou is Love in Action! Shine On Sister!"

- Laura Duksta, Ambassador of Love and New York Times Bestselling Author of *I Love You More* and *You Are a Gift to the World*

"Lilou Mace's *I Had No Money and I Liked It* reminds us that even those of us who succeed are human – and how beautiful and perfect our human-ness really is."

- Danielle MacKinnon Intuitive and author of the upcoming book, *Animal Soul Contracts*.

"At this time of intense planetary change, Lilou Mace's book *I Had No Money and I Liked It* is more than a personal journal on how to co-create with the new energy, it's an important book that has the power to light up the journey for decades to come. With the same pioneering energy that Lilou demonstrates in everything she takes on, she now opens a new path that challenges our relationship with money and the concept of feeling secure inside and outside. Let's allow ourselves to be inspired by this generous testimony because it is together, and not on our own, that we embark on the new Earth, with new ways of being, thinking and doing."

- Danielle Clermont, Intuitive Astrologer and Author

"Lilou Mace is one of those persons who wants her life to be an adventure in many dimensions and turns up at the right place at the right time for manifesting her mission. This requires a kind of spiritual courage, or in other words, faith in higher providence that we all need in these times. Her books are well written accounts of where life may take you if you are willing to let go."

- Carl Johan Calleman, Ph.D. author of *The Purposeful Universe* and expert on the Mayan Calendar

"Lilou Mace took a leap of faith in herself, others and the Law of Attraction when she dared to live her life trusting the Universal laws. Choosing the direction of trust and self empowerment has repaid her over and over in many different and sometimes surprising ways. Her strength lies in her determination to keep walking in that direction no matter how many curves and run about she encounters. She embodies the attributes of the spiritual warrior and the warmth of a true host. She is welcoming, curious and friendly towards others and life in general. She is bold and enthusiastic. Trough the experiences, related in this episode of her juicy tour, she express true connection with self, zero point and love of self and others. Her life of no compromise, is a life of discipline and passion. The passion, to live fully on her sacred essential path and the discipline, to continually seeking its manifestation."

- Kishori Aird, author of *DNA Demystified*, *Essence* and other books.

"Lilou Mace is not a woman who just talks about synchronicity, open heartedness and the wonder of life's events. She is someone who experiences it! And she does so with humor and with grace!"

- Layne Dalfen dream analyst, Founder of The Dream Interpretation Center in Montreal, and author of *Dreams Do Come True; Decoding Your Dreams To Discover Your Full Potential.*

"Lilou Mace's *I Had No Money and I Liked It* is a wonderful, exciting, fascinating exploration of the power of faith and synchronicity. Written in the form of a journal, we follow Lilou day to day as she faces the challenges of living in the flow of synchronicity, giving herself to what feels authentic and vital to her life. We see her moments of doubt, we feel her uncertainties, and we witness her growing faith in what she is doing. As her faith grows, the world opens up to her in a way that is miraculous. No other book could possibly show you what it's like to move into this space, and what it truly feels like. For spiritual progress is never as easy as it seems afterwards, and this book reminds us of the actual day to day struggles and triumphs. For these reasons – and many others – it will inspire you. You want to know what it feels like to let go and trust? These pages will show you as no other book can. Then the next questions are – Will you let go? Can you trust? Lilou will show you the way. Lilou is a true pioneer, and for her courage and determination we will always be grateful."

- Dr Allan Hunter, author: *The Path of Synchronicity* and other books

"As Lilou shares her shift of conscisousness leading her to an open heart she realises the real abundance of life. Lilou's vibrant spirit is infectuous in this book."

- Sonia Choquette, NY Times Best selling author of *Ask Your Guides*, *Trust Your Vibes* and other books

"Lilou's book supports not only the human experience, but the joyous reality of what each person is here to fully manifest on the planet at this time for their truest and highest nature. The gift this author has given to each reader, is the simple understanding that we can be our true selves in these turbulent times. We can shine our light in service for the greater good of humanity, to mirror back to them what is possible, if we live our highest goals and dreams, and make them a reality instead of a potentiality. Lilou is a gifted communicator, she shares with the world, humanity's ability to breathe Truth into form by allowing us through her personal sharing to be vulnerable and true, while listening and following our highest soul's purpose. She is talented in her ability to teach and gives us the language of purposeful intent to each show up and be who we really are. I highly recommend that you read this book because it will change your thinking into positive results that produce the actual manifestation of your life's purpose. Lilou is a fully human embodiment of love, inspiration and freedom, she teaches through her example, how to live your highest dream."

- Mirabai Devi, new paradigm spiritual teacher and author of *Samadhi: Essence of the Divine*

FOREWORD

As we are leaving the present age, the Age of Reason, we are entering the next age, the Age of Whole-ism. There has never been a time like this at any previous point in human history. With all the changes that have occurred, never before has every single one of the major pillars upon which civilization is built been threatened. Now, each of those pillars is in the process of tumbling down; from the fundamental structures of the churches to the trust one has in the governmental and the financial systems. We can no longer reason our way through the challenges and crises with which we are being confronted.

We are the people who are living through the breakdown of one world, the familiar one, and the rise of one that has not yet been built.

Lilou is someone who clearly understands that the old form of Reason has come to the end of its usefulness. She opens her heart and follows the guidance of her soul by tapping into the present moment. She adjusts to the world that is changing at the speed of light and draws from a level of creativity and flexibility that can only come from the Higher Self. She inspires us with her interviews and reminds us of the same simple yet beautiful, eternal truths that the Buddha and Jesus taught when they both said: "The teachings are in you." Lilou reveals their teachings to us when she shows us, through example, that the real Law of Attraction works through people. As she further opens her heart, she encounters other people who live from an open heart; people who inspire her, support her and love her. She is no different than you and me, but through her work, she accommodates light. She understands the abundance of loving your life and treasuring your greatness and she makes it practical by taking action in the physical world. She shows us that if you have the courage and the determination to live from your heart, the Graces start opening up, like flowers that start blooming in you, when perhaps you didn't even know they were there…

This book is a river full of vibrant, sparkling grace and practical wisdom.

It powerfully demonstrates that, even though we sometimes have no money and times are hard, we can all navigate through those waters by tapping into the wisdom of an open heart. Lilou shows us that we can't meditate in order to open our hearts. Life shatters the heart open and with that, it makes room in our lives for other people with open hearts.

Lilou has a healer's heart and through her work, she is healing the world.

Baptist de Pape
Producer, *The Power of the Heart*
The Netherlands, September 2011

AUTHOR'S NOTE

This book is about what it takes to be free, what it takes to develop that core muscle inside of us that is rock solid, that feels secure, grounded in reality, and connected to our higher self no matter what our outside circumstances are. It is about reconnecting to the true abundance, to life beyond blame, so we can live a juicy life—a life where our essence shines out every day, unconditionally.

I believe that human beings have extraordinary potential to live great lives. All of us. This can happen by listening to life with an open heart, taking inspired action, and giving of ourselves unconditionally. This can happen by directing our hearts toward what we really want, while being grateful and appreciative for everything on the way. But I think most of all, we shouldn't get stuck in the lessons or in the past. We have to do what *feels good* because I really believe that is one of the main indicators of where we should be heading.

Here is the plan: The plan is to move forward, to accept the lessons we receive, to accept the challenges, and to accept 100% responsibility for our lives. It is to take the next inspiring step, to shift our energy (negative thoughts to positive thoughts if needed), and to find the balance between having faith and surrendering. It is to be out there fully and authentically. It is to come from the center, grounded, passionate point inside of us that is calm, powerful, and understands all that is, beyond reasons.

And yes, co-creator, we're going to make it! I'm so happy that you are taking part in this journey with me. I'm so happy because I know that, if you're reading this, your life is transforming. It is time to enjoy the ride, learn the lessons that are needed, and help others along the way. We're all interconnected. We're all magnificent and powerful co-creators. That I know. And I hope you can acknowledge that within yourself, because that acknowledgment is one of the biggest favors you can do for yourself.

I believe in you. I believe in what you are doing. I believe you have unique talents, and it is time to let them shine.

CHAPTER 1: IT IS BECOMING AN OBSESSION

May 2nd 2009

MONEY IS LIKE WATER

I'm so moved, touched, and inspired right now. I just finished a run. As I'm walking back from Hyde Park, I am listening to one of Lynn Twist's tracks on money and I am in tears. She has just described one of her fundraising experiences. It is so beautiful how she describes money as being like water that just flows through us and how it is a carrier for more things to happen in the world. I'm clear that it's my duty to let money flow through my life so I can do many wonderful things with it. I just know that this is possible. I'm moved by Lynn Twist's story.

WE HAVE A SOUL, MONEY DOESN'T

Lynn also said that money has no soul but we do, and with that, we can do so much. That is the commitment, the focus, and the force behind this book. I want to help people and eventually expand that help by starting a foundation to make it possible for kids all over the world to discover new countries and new cultures; to give them the chance to travel at a young age. By doing this, they will learn about different cultures, and it will reduce ignorance in the world and the fear that some people experience when they meet others who look and act differently than they do.

I am in tears now. My God, people seeing me probably think I'm nuts. Here I am in the middle of London, walking and crying. But I don't care. I so much want to make a difference in the world, and I realize that I can. I think that's why I am in tears—because I'm in touch with my soul right now, in this very second, and I want to remember this moment forever.

May 3rd

BONDING TIME

I love interviewing book authors. I just interviewed Ann Gadd. It was so amazing. She's based in South Africa. When you think about it, I'm based in London, and here we are miles apart and having this amazing conversation. The interview was a lot of fun. At times, we were laughing together. You have to understand that it's not really my style to just hang out with people and spend quality bonding time. I have to say that's one of my weaknesses. I spend a lot of time on my own and do not always take the time to really know others intimately. I think I am scared of it. But with Ann, we were very relaxed, making fun of each other, and having a great time. We did four different video interviews that I will be posting on YouTube.

BEYOND THE MONEY

In the process of bonding with authors, I am also learning so much. In the weeks to come, I will be interviewing them after reading their books. In so many ways, those experiences are going to contribute to making my own book a success. I am doing this because I love it, and yes, I am able to make some money doing these interviews. But there are other rewards that also come from these encounters, and they are just phenomenal. I think it is all part of the equation. I'm learning so much from each of these authors. I look forward to sharing those author interviews with you on YouTube. Speak to you soon, co-creator!

May 4th

FABULOUSLY ON PURPOSE

I cannot even express how much fun it is to be on purpose. Today is a bank holiday in England, so I took the time to run. I did a long run since I'm training for the half marathon in mid-October over in Palma de Majorca. It's just so juicy, you know. I was just watching a bit of TV, and I ended up seeing a show called *The Fabulous Life.* It's funny because tomorrow I'm being interviewed by Sandy Grason in Los Angeles on her radio talk show *The Road to Fabulous*. I love those winks of the Universe!

DRESSED FOR SUCCESS

I feel more grounded here. I think one of the reasons is because I don't watch those E! Entertainment type shows that make you dream, but do not really ground you. However, *The Fabulous Life* show reminded me that I can share my first fashion manifestation story on Sandy Grason's talk show. It came about after I met Jeminee Solanki, a young and upcoming Indian fashion designer in London. While we were out clubbing one night, she recognized me from YouTube and asked me to wear her dresses. How cool is that!

So I just sent Jeminee an email. I told her I that I look forward to meeting her and said I will be mentioning her in the radio interview. Sandy Grason and I haven't been in communication much lately. She is now living in Colorado, and it will be so good to speak with her. She's awesome, has great energy, and I do miss her.

It's funny to see how everything is really coming together. I look forward to being dressed for success! I just love it when you allow the Universe to take care of the details. I said to myself a few days ago that I wanted to attract a new wardrobe, and here it is! I met a fashion designer, and I'll soon be wearing the dresses she has created.

A PERFECT MATCH

Hopefully, I will be a good fit for Jeminiee's fashion creations. What's beautiful about the Law of Attraction is that, usually, when things like that happen, it's a perfect match. You don't even need to think twice. Usually it's even beyond your expectations. We'll see here...but I look forward to stepping it up. I have to say that my wardrobe is a bit dull. So I added some trendy and fashionable clothes on my vision board. I am lucky to be 1m81 (6 foot) tall, so I can wear some unusual things. I never really allowed myself to do so. I feel now that I am being on purpose; I will be able to put my best foot forward. As time goes on, I want to attract other fashion designers that will want me to be seen wearing their latest collection. How fun would that be? It is also one of my "girl's" dreams.

ONE OPPORTUNITY LEADS TO ANOTHER

I just received an email from Thierry Bogliolo. He is the first publisher I have as a client. I am interviewing his authors, and I am still in shock that I am being paid to learn from and interview these people.

So, bit by bit, I'm gathering information that has the potential to open up opportunities to attract more money and lead to interviews with even more people. I really like how all this is taking shape. I am really enjoying these interviews and have now figured out how to record them by webcam on Skype so I can do a lot more of them.

LOVING WHAT I DO AND MAGNETIZING MORE OF IT

I just love to interview people. I learn so much from the experience.

I have the chance to meet so many wonderful people, and I can share my experience on YouTube. So it is a win-win situation for everyone. The more people I interview, the more my videos are out there, and the more people learn and grow. Again, I think this is all part of my intention of becoming a bestselling author—making an amazing living doing what I love and allowing my dreams to unfold. It's absolutely amazing.

May 5th

GUIDED & CREATIVE VISUALIZATIONS

Good morning! I just started the day with a visualization, that I have recorded. I've been visualizing myself on the couch of a famous UK TV show talking with the host about my book and sharing some of the inspirational stories that are featured in it. In the visualization, I am feeling the excitement of having the camera 'on air' and the news being spread all over the country. I am also feeling the excitement of uploading the video of my appearance on that famous UK TV show on YouTube and sharing my excitement with people about the experience as if it has already happened.

A SYNCHRONICITY

Right now, I'm reading *The Six Archetypes of Love: From Innocent to Magician* by Dr. Allan G. Hunter. On the first page, I read a quote from Dr. Pat Baccili, who is the host of the *Dr. Pat Show* and I'm thinking, "This name rings a bell. Why is that?" So I look up information on Dr. Pat Baccili and find my answer. Of course, I recognized Pat because I was interviewed by her a couple of years ago about the 100-Day Reality Challenge on her radio show. So I immediately sent Pat an email to ask if she would be interested in interviewing me about *I Lost My Job and I Liked It*. She's absolutely a lovely lady, and with the subject of my book being so timely, she could very well be interested in having me as a guest. I'm grateful to be reminded of Dr. Pat right now by simply opening to the first page of Allan Hunter's book.

VOICE IT OUT

I am so grateful for the recording device on my iPhone. I think it is a very powerful tool, and I encourage you to audio record your own thoughts. Speaking your thoughts, intentions, feelings, dreams, goals, or fears out loud really gives them tremendous power. As I record my thoughts, one idea leads to another and to another and it just keeps unfolding. It helps me stay in the flow of things. I think video blogging is even more powerful as not only do you voice it out, but you also broadcast it to others, and receive support from the outside, which is so important. However, it is a big time commitment to upload a video blog every day. Voice memos do not take as much time. I record them every day, a few times a day. Sometimes I will record a voice memo when I am on my way to a meeting or if I have a thought that I want to expand on at a later time.

For me, I think there is great value in recording your thoughts; speaking them out loud. Whether it's through video or audio recording, there is something very special about doing it. Journaling is great too, but not always easy to do while on the go.

BRINGING THINGS BACK INTO BALANCE

I feel that Life brings us naturally back into balance, when we allow it to. For example, I received a note from the Indian publisher letting me know that they are not interested in publishing my book. I know that this means something better will be manifesting, but part of me thought for a moment, *"Well maybe this book is not as good as I thought, because otherwise, they would have accepted it and been delighted to take it on."* But I'm not going to give into that thought because that would just create more negative thoughts and, sooner or later, I would have dug myself a rabbit hole, and how far and deep would it go?

So I'm not going into that spiral, definitely not, because I want to live a powerful story here. Receiving the email has brought me back into balance and grounded me. It serves its purpose and helps to balance my energy, which was getting over-excited. This reminds me of the Point Zero concept that Dr. John Demartini referred to in one of his lectures. The idea is not to get into the big highs, as they will be followed by big lows. Instead, you find an intermediate place (the point zero) where you're closer to your true self; you're grounded, in balance, aware, and present to the moment.

BIG HIGH

I received one of my first larger payments for interviewing book authors. WOW! I feel very grateful and excited. I cannot help but think of even more money coming in now. I am on a big high. I had £300 ($490) in my bank account.

I feel that everything is possible. I feel freedom from which I can desire and allow in all of the abundance of the Universe. But this is not coming from greed or a desire for accumulation or any of that. It is because it quiets my worries to be compensated for what I'm bringing into the world. I'm opening that valve and allowing it to happen so I look forward to attracting more.

May 6th

SHIFTING ENERGY

My mind is a bit in scarcity mode right now. I'm just looking at things and saying to myself, "Oh, how can you pretend that you're going to become a bestselling author?" and "That's going to require lots of promotion." and "How are you going to do this?" and "There are countless numbers of books out there." and "Who are you to be at the top?" and "Is your book worth it?" I'm having this train of thought like, "You're going down." So I'm just going to take a moment to clear my thoughts as I have some interviews to do very soon with a number of book authors. I'm just going to stop and visit the local park right now. There is a little bit of sunshine today, but I'm going to cover myself up to make sure I don't get cold because the air is pretty chilly. I'm going to go take a blanket and a cushion with me to the park where I will read a book and take the time to re-center, re-energize, and recharge my battery. I need to shift my energy right now.

THE PATH DOWN

I think I know what triggered my earlier thoughts and why I was starting to go down the rabbit hole; having one negative thought after another. I went online to buy a ticket to go to France on the weekend of the 14th of May. I had been taking low-cost airlines to Nantes to visit my parents. That way, I could get a ticket for under £100 ($163.35). I didn't really enjoy those flights, those big loud colors and the fact that I had to travel outside of London to catch the planes, but it was inexpensive. Each time I was traveling with those airlines, I was annoyed by the fact that they would add a hand luggage fee, another for food, and yet another for extra luggage and so forth. It was not the most pleasurable experience, but I always traveled that way because it was less money. However, today I went online to book a flight with one of those airlines and found that they no longer operate between

London and Nantes. No more cheap flights! Oh no!

BETTER EXPERIENCE, HIGHER VIBRATION

After that discovery, I did an online search and ended up on the Air France website. I decided to book a flight with them not worrying about the price which, as it turned out, was still very reasonable considering the departure is very soon. The good news is that the flight is actually leaving from central London. So that means I won't have to take a train to the airport, which cost me £35 ($56.61) roundtrip, and because I'm flying with Air France, I probably won't have to pay an additional fee for the hand luggage. So ultimately, the flight is pretty much the same price, and I'm gaining time because it's departing from the London City Airport, which is much closer.

The experience of flying with Air France is definitely much better. The arrival and departure times are better too. Everything about it makes me feel good and much more comfortable. So I started relaxing and stopped worrying about the cost. It is just better all around. It is interesting that, with my earlier thoughts of scarcity, I had not even considered looking at this option before. Now I feel really happy. My vibration is much higher.

BREAKING THE NEGATIVE CYCLE

You know how it goes...one negative thought attracts another and another and you have got to stop the inner dialog really fast when it starts to go that way. The good thing is that it works the same with positive thoughts! It is very important that we recognize negative thoughts when they start and stop everything we're doing, breathe deeply, do anything it takes to break the negative thought cycle, and get back into the flow.

Now that I am in the park and I'm relaxing my mind, I'm able to see the pattern and shift it. I have shifted my thoughts to those of happiness and abundance. I repeat to myself, *"I am becoming a bestselling author."* In doing that, I am once again living in the moment and visualizing how it will feel to have my book *I Lost My Job and I Liked It* at number one in top sales on Amazon.

I am breathing again.

BEING CHILDLIKE

What's wonderful is that I am relaxing in a park that is in the middle of London. It's a private park that can only be accessed by the people that live around it. This is quite common in the richer neighborhoods of London. It is a truly special feeling to be out in nature, especially when you live in an apartment with no garden! Today what's different about this park is that I'm surrounded by children. They are playing and having fun. Observing them is quite interesting. They are being so creative in their play; not worrying about falling down or looking stupid. They are totally going with the flow. I think there's so much to learn from the spontaneity of children; the joy in their eyes, their sparkle, witnessing them falling down and standing right back up again. I want the next weeks and months of my life to be very playful. I want to have fun, to be childlike. I want to allow the Universe to guide me and life to flow through me every day.

FINDING THE KID IN ME

I'm thankful for this moment where I have the privilege of learning from children. I want to find the kid in me and not take life so seriously. I want to be playful. I have a friend who really captures that childlike wonder. His name is Hank Andries. I think he is 64 years old. He has been running many successful businesses. One of the things that I admire most about Hank, apart from his being available to help at any time and give good advice, is that he has a great sense of humor. He is always playful and joking about things. I think it's important, even in business, to be like that; just like a kid. I think that is the very thing that makes him successful. He is so joyful and fun to be around.

Of course, sometimes Hank can get on my nerves because I don't know when I should take him seriously. He just laughs at things. When I'm pissed off, stressed or troubled, he just keeps laughing and giggling like a five year old. What a beautiful example of childlike wonder he is to have in my life. I wanted to mention him because he is an inspiration. He is an adult who reminds me of these kids playing. It makes me think that age doesn't really mean anything. It is something I'm looking forward to learning more about on this journey.

COMPARING MYSELF WITH OTHERS

When I compare myself with others, there are doubts that crawl back in. That's what happened earlier when I saw Jerry and Esther Hicks' new book on the Law of Attraction, and I started losing confidence in myself. I told myself in that moment: *"Jerry and Esther Hicks sell millions of copies, forget about the success of mine."* And you see, in seconds, I just went into that whole loop on how it's not worth it, how I should not write a new book. But I caught those thoughts, and then I was able to shift that thinking to *"No, I'm still going to write it."* I am in the park enjoying the time and the beautiful weather. It feels like summer. It's lovely.

Oh, by the way, I found someone to sell the rights of my book in all countries, and I have possibly found a publisher. So I'm working on that, co-creator. It's manifesting. It's happening. The juice is flowing. I'm guided.

May 10th

A NEW CONNECTION

It's amazing how life works out. Here is the email that Dr. Allan

Hunter, who I have interviewed, forwarded to me:

"Dear Sir Hunter,

We are a group of independent filmmakers who currently have joined forces to create a documentary on the fascinating workings of the heart. We would like to ask you whether we could interview you for our documentary. We saw you on Lilou Macé's YouTube channel explaining the Cinderella story, and we would love to use it in our documentary.
Kind regards,
Baptist de Pape"

It feels so rewarding that Allan is thanking me for interviewing him and that the interview has helped him to connect to another project. I feel very, very blessed and see the huge amounts of energy and power that the Universe has if we just allow it to unfold. I'm ready to receive.

May 13th

FIRST COPIES OF MY BOOK BEING PRINTED

I just received an email this morning from David Royffe in which he shared a juicy synchronicity with me. While in London yesterday, he found a copy of my book already printed and displayed on a shelf in a Blackwell book shop and purchased it. I had no idea that print-on-demand companies were already making my book available for printing, much less that a printed copy could be found in a book shop. In fact, I'm still waiting for my proofed copy from Lightning Source to arrive via DHL delivery today. Now, thanks to the email from David, I know that it is possible to get copies of my book from the Blackwell book shop (or another shop that has a print-on-demand machine) before I fly out to France tomorrow. I'm delighted to see how things are unfolding. David "attracted" a copy of my book and tells me that he's enjoying it so much, he cannot put it down! What makes this so extraordinary is that, officially, the book is not even for sale in the UK yet. Wow!

AN ENCOURAGING MESSAGE

Okay, I just received the following message from David Royffe in which he tells me the full story of finding and purchasing a copy of my book:

"I only heard of it and found it because I searched and found the print- on-demand espresso machine in Blackwell bookstore. I had not heard of you or your book till I saw the book on the rack of the machine booth. There was just one copy of your book on the rack and I chose to buy it. Firstly because I wanted an example of a print-on-demand (product) and also, your book stood out as interesting and relevant to me. I have thousands of books at home and I have found that books have the habit of finding me... Anyway, I was so determined to buy your book having quickly scanned the cover and title and learning a bit about you, that's what I did."

Thank you, David! I'm going with the flow and one step at a time.

A BLESSING IN BEING HACKED?

I just found out that it was possible to download my eBook for free! Did someone hack it? At the beginning I was quite upset. I thought "*Oh okay, somebody posted my eBook online for free so I'm not going to receive income from it.*" And then quickly after that thought came to me, it changed. "*Actually, this may be really cool because this way I can get my message out to many more people, and the more people searching for the book and reading it, the better.*" I know it sounds strange because, yes, I do want to make income from the book. I want the book to become a bestseller. But I have heard that many bestselling authors actually offer a free version of their work early on. This is because, even if people are passing around an eBook at first, the more people who read your work, the more people there will be who want the printed version of it. I like to read the "real" book. There is something really cool and special about it. We'll see how this all works out. For now, I don't feel threatened by what the hacker did. Instead, I find the concept quite interesting, and I am not going to worry about it.

MONEY IS ENERGY

I think we all have some misconceptions about the nature of money and how it can flow. Money is clearly energy. There is a great book by author Stuart Wilde called *The Little Money Bible*. Deepak Chopra has written some great books on money, and so have Jerry and Esther Hicks.

ALLOWING MONEY TO FLOW IN

I'm just checking on the funds I have in the bank. Because I travel around quite a bit, I have different accounts; one in the UK, one in the US, and another in France. But sometimes, part of me just doesn't want to look at the balance in those accounts because I don't want to worry. On the other hand, I think I worry more when I don't exactly know my financial situation. Right now, I don't have much money showing on my accounts. Still, I feel grounded. I feel secure. I feel like I'm spending conservatively and using good judgment. I'm able to pay my bills, fly to France to see my parents this weekend. The Universe is taking care of my needs. I'm allowing the money to flow in.

As I had said in my previous book, I didn't know that money would come from interviewing people, but as of today, that is my main source of income. Yet now and then, I have little financial fears that come up, and I think, *"Okay, but how about next month?"*

But, I stop those thoughts by focusing on the abundance of this world. I think about the emails that I'm receiving; the support I get from the community. I remember that the videos I create and those created by others are truly an example of how important it is to stay in the flow, to just let things happen, to allow life to unfold knowing that I will be taken care of. I'm not sitting on my couch and doing nothing. I am dedicated to living my dream. I definitely have a burning desire to make this happen.

Talking about money, I just looked at my US bank account, which I don't often check, and it shows that there has been a money transfer from Google Adsense, as I am a Youtube partner. Some money has come in. Alright, it's flowing. It's flowing. Keep it flowing.

Boy, I cannot wait to hold my book in my hands. Where is the DHL person?

VIBRANT FOODS

It's now around noon. I'm going to have one of my favorite foods, avocado. It is so rich, so good, so nurturing. I believe raw foods raise our energy levels and vibrations. I'm going to have the avocado with some kale, little spring onions, pumpkin seeds, wonderful organic cider vinegar and some juicy, juicy other ingredients. I'm so excited, co-creator, that my book is already making a difference!

A NEW STEP IN THE ADVENTURE

It's now 1:30pm and I just received the proof copy of my self-published book from DHL and it looks beautiful. It's the new 8" x 5" format! It looks absolutely stunning and amazing. I am so proud, so grateful. I'm going to accept the proofed copy right now. This is the first book, co-creator, that I am proofing, printing, and distributing. How cool!

The book looks fabulous with such a glossy cover. It is unbelievable. I'm clicking on "proof acceptance" and then on "submit." Yeah, that's it. Now I'm going to email the client service representative to make sure she knows that all is good and ready to go. This is so exciting. I'm bringing the final proofed copy of the book with me to France! Oh, I'm so proud. Thank you, thank you, thank you, Life. Thank you for making this happen. Thank you for the amazing adventure it has been so far and the wonderful things that are now unfolding with this book. I am so, so happy and delighted. Thank you so much.

A DREAM COMING TRUE!

Alright, co-creator, this feels so good. This is all becoming real. I have just ordered the first box of 57 books. I was tempted to order more, but having a limited number of books will help me to only distribute them to the right people. I will also start selling the books and I just cannot wait. I think the other copies of the book are going to arrive tomorrow. I will be in France, so when I come back on Monday, I will have the copies waiting for me. This is very, very exciting. It's like a dream coming true.

Although I have already had an early copy of the book in my hand, this one is the final version. It is the same version that will be in the hands of millions of people! It looks good. It shines. The book was created with love and you can definitely feel its vibrancy. It's got an amazing energy to it. A wonderful designer, did the cover using some of the photos taken by Jack Latimer, the 22-year-old photography student that I hired to do the photo shoot. When I went through the photographs Jack shot to select the one I wanted on the cover, I ended up choosing Picture number 77; the same number as my birth year: 1977. When I saw it, I just knew it was the one.

FEELING GOOD

Ahhhhh...I'm listening right now to Michael Bublé's recording of "Feeling Good." I love that song. This music makes me feel so good. I'm downloading it from iTunes, and I have also created a ring tone from it to inspire me to feel good more often. Songs like this are such a powerful tool in reminding us to shift our energy and be in the flow. It's just beautiful and amazing. But now I should pack before I meet my new friend, Brian. He is a beautiful,

beautiful human being. I just love London. I love this city. It is full of such gorgeous, wonderful people.

May 14th

STEPPING IT UP

I'm at the London City Airport ready to fly to France. It is the first time I am flying out of this airport. London has five airports: Heathrow, Gatwick, Stansted, Luton, and the London City Airport. Well, this really feels good. It feels like flying business class as it is a small, elegant airport and a lot of business people fly out of London from here. I am flying out on a small plane. I am traveling with Air France instead of those low-cost airlines with big yellow and orange planes. I got this plane ticket, and I can tell you, *this* is the way I always want to fly. It inspires me to do more traveling. I had a late night last night. I went to bed at 2:30am and I had to wake up at 6:00am, but I had a wonderful time meeting Grant, who was introduced to me by my other friend. We had an incredible conversation, and Grant taught me a great lesson about being bold, audacious, and just daring to do whatever it takes to make things happen. I'm definitely taking this on, co-creator. Okay, it is time to fly to France. See you there!

HAVE WE REACHED OUR FULL HUMAN POTENTIAL?

Bonjour! I am in Nantes, France, co-creator! There is an interesting conversation on the French radio about how robots are catching up to human beings. They are saying on the show that we are making them more and more independent to the point where they will soon be conscious. I am so not sure about that! One of the speakers is saying that we have reached our full human potential. I disagree with him because I think we are only starting. I want to continue on my quest for tapping into the immense potential that exists. However, at this moment, I must shift my focus to the road ahead. These French people are crazy when they drive, including me! See you later, co-creator.

VISION VIDEO

I'm going to do a vision video specifically for the book. I'm going to pick up some digital images, animate them into a video, and get into the feeling place. Hmmm, I like that idea. It is another little tool.

CALLED INTO IMMEDIATE ACTION

I'm laughing because, when I have an idea, I just love doing things right away! I think this part of my personality really works for me because, when I get inspired, I act very quickly. Otherwise, I might end up just getting excited and not doing anything about it. So I like making things happen now!

ASKING FOR GUIDANCE AND RECEIVING IT

I am ready to go to bed and ask for guidance throughout the night. I'll wake up with some new ideas and feel refreshed, creative, powerful, productive, and prosperous. Good night. Bonne nuit.

May 15th

Hello, co-creator. Today is Friday and, just as I asked, I woke up with an idea…a fun little idea. I am going to have people from all around the world take their pictures with my book.

IT IS ABOUT THE MESSAGE, NOT THE BOOK

It's interesting what we can attract and how powerful we are. I'm always so surprised. One of the things that I've declared I will focus on is getting the media involved with my book and finding a way to get mentioned in the press. Tonight I am at my mother's house watching a TV show dealing with how unknown people became famous. There are some beautiful stories showing people who have fought for a cause and gone beyond the ordinary to live their life missions and inspire others.

This is starting to wake up some ideas in me. I want to help people learn how to attract their dream jobs, but to do that, I must first focus on the message rather than on wanting to sell the book. The book is a tool for me to get the message out there and inspire millions of people. However, to meaningfully help people, I must get the message out now. Once I share the message, the book will sell itself.

So I have to start thinking outside of the box and find a radical, groundbreaking way to inspire media attention. I'm grateful for this book taking a bit more time to get printed and published because that extra time has allowed things to shape up a little bit differently and mature. There are no coincidences in life. This is happening right now because there is something I am meant to understand; a better, bigger way to approach the book so it can become a bestseller.

May 16th

RE-CREATING

I have to say that I'm quite intrigued and excited. The Law of Attraction is powerful, but you have to pay attention to what you want, co-creator. For instance, right now I am feeling a bit fearful, so I have to calm down, breathe in, and recreate by doing some meditation or visualization.

AUDACITY

Life is definitely showing me a sign here. I am seeing examples of audacity everywhere. It came up the other day in my conversation with Grant. And now the cover of *Paris Match* (a famous French magazine) is featuring an "audacious" picture of Sophie Marceau for the promotion of her new movie. Yesterday on TV I saw people that were described as bold and audacious. There is *Audacity of Hope*, of course, a beautiful book by Barack Obama that I read partially when I was in Chicago. The audacity theme keeps reappearing in my life. I think it is a reminder that I need to be audacious. I'm going to embrace audacity (pronounced: aw-da-city), but I want to learn more about its true meaning.

When I checked online, I find this definition:
1. Fearless, daring.
2. Bold or insolent.
3. An act or instance of intrepidity or insolence; heedlessness.

I get the message! I'm open to audacious thoughts, boldness, and following the lead. Yes, I am ready.

May 18th

COMING TOGETHER. A MIRACLE!

This is my last day in France. It was very special yesterday because my mom and dad met for real in a normal context. Wow, it was the first time since I was 12 years old that I saw them speaking to each other. I thought my dad was going to back out at the last minute. We met at the "Jumping International" of La Bauble, and we had a fabulous time. We didn't spend too much time together, maybe an hour, but we talked. It was the perfect set-up; the horses, my mom, my dad, and me. I was so very, very happy. I also showed my dad a copy of my book. I was proud.

EARLY LIFE COMMITMENTS

I love horses. I can't even begin to tell you how much I love them. You see horses have always been my passion. I did jumpings from the age of eight until I was 18. So when I see horses, it actually reminds me of one of my early life commitments. It was that, one day, I would have horses of my own at home and be able to ride them after work. As we all know, horses cost a lot of money. So just being in that whole atmosphere reminded me how much I love horses and how important my early life commitment was to me back then and still is today.

OBSESSING ABOUT MONEY

I am sending those burning desires, rocket after rocket after rocket, even in my sleep. My desire to make money is even greater than before. It has become an obsession now. I have to say, it's not that I'm frustrated about money at the moment. I'm very content with what I have.

Listening to my mom describe the type of house that she wishes to have inspires me. She wants to buy land around here and build a new house. She also wants to change her kitchen. I mean, you know how we are with our parents. We just want to please them and give back to them for all they have given us. So what drives my desire even more is the thought of my parents.

Yes, co-creator, I'm focused…I'm there. But for right now, I am here and it is time for me to get started with my run. I'll speak to you later.

May 19th

FEELING THE FLOW!

I'm back in London. This morning I'm heading to DHL to hopefully pick up the first box of 57 books that I have ordered. I just took the Tube and am now heading to DHL Express, which should be around here. Thank God for GPS. Alright, this is exciting!

Yes! I have 57 books. Well, actually 55, because I gave two away at the DHL store. I just couldn't resist giving one to the guy behind the counter and another to a client picking up his stuff. They wanted the books signed so I signed both books. Now I officially have 55 books to carry, and I am attracting a taxi cab to go back because the box is quite heavy. It is so exciting, exciting, exciting! It feels like Christmas!

FROM LAWYER TO MOVIE MAKER OF THE HEART

I just talked through Skype with Baptist de Pape for the first time. I originally connected with him through interviewing Fred Master and Dr. Allan Hunter. Apparently, Baptist has been watching my videos for a while. He's producing a movie on the power of the heart and has been interviewing spiritual world leaders such as Desmond Tutu, Jane Goodall, Gregg Braden, and Deepak Chopra. He has also recently connected with Dr. Allan Hunter who is a person I've been interviewing.

Baptist has so much wisdom, and he just shared many of his ideas with me. We just talked and talked and talked. We could have easily talked all day long, and I'm sure this is not the last time. Oprah is one of his inspirations, too. He told me that after seeing the Oprah Winfrey seminar online with Eckhart Tolle on *A New*

Earth, he was inspired to walk away from a job as a successful lawyer in Holland and become a filmmaker. How courageous! He is producing and directing a movie on the wisdom of the heart. He said that one day he went to this park outside of his place, meditated, and started feeling his heart opening up to the powerful desire to get this project started. What was amazing is that we just had this conversation and discovered that we have so many people in common, so we can help each other.

DON'T WORRY, JUST TRUST YOUR SOUL

Baptist is all about helping others and just reminded me not to worry. He said that it's important to trust your soul, the Universe, and consciousness because, as Deepak Chopra would say, we have extraordinary human potential. Our potential is in our soul, and we don't need to do anything but trust and allow. It's really about being in a state of connection with the soul. It is a state of being in which things unfold and happen magically.

It was such a wonderful reminder to speak with such a person. We were both born the same year, 1977. I just feel so blessed to have connected with Baptist. The main message here was don't worry. Don't worry…just trust your soul, which I'm going to do right now.

SHARING THE JOY

I'm about to ship out a few of my books. I'm going to ship one to Navin Chandaria, a great friend and mentor from Toronto, and one to Gerry Hillman, the person who designed the inside of my book. Another copy is going to Dr. Allan Hunter. He is an absolutely amazing person. I'm also going to send three copies of the book to Baptist because he knows publishers in Belgium and in Holland, and he is going to pass those copies along for me.

I'm sending one copy of the book to the "Oprah Winfrey Show" and one to Marc Holland, who did the cover of my book. I'm also sending one to Thierry Borgiolo, a publisher from Findhorn Press. I'm sending one to Genevieve Materne, who is the person who hired me in the first place, which brought me to the UK as internet marketing director and where I ultimately lost my job. It was that series of events that made this adventure possible. I'm sending one to Megan Castran. She is a CCOR member who lives in Australia and is absolutely phenomenal. I am also sending the ten promised copies to Eric Swanepoel, the editor of my first book.

SO MUCH FUN!

This was so much fun. I sent out about 20 copies of my book

to different people all around the world. I also promised copies of the book to other people while I was at the post office. I was served and helped by a postal employee named Kalinah, and she was so thrilled and excited about the title of the book, that I ended up giving her a copy. It was amazing. There was this big buzz in the whole post office, and I just had so much fun! Kalinah was especially excited to see that I was sending a copy of the book to the "Oprah Winfrey Show." She took particular care with that package! Later on, when I had to go back to the post office, Kalinah told me, *"Yeah, the book is so promising. You know the title's so catchy and all of us just hate our jobs here."* And I was just laughing because she was so spontaneous, so honest, and so great, and that's what the whole book is about. She really created a buzz right then and there. It reminded me how much potential the book has, and I truly believe it is going to take off by itself. I'm just letting things happen.

SURPRISED BY LIFE

I cannot believe that my ex-boss, Peter Gould, commented on the video where I sang my own version of the Katy Perry song, "I Kissed a Girl (and I Liked It)" changing the lyrics to fit my book, *I Lost My Job and I Liked It.* That was so funny! I'm surprised how everyone is loving and enjoying that particular video. I definitely created it with a lot of energy. It has been over a month since it appeared on YouTube when a friend posted it as a joke, and the response is amazing. (Smile) This is fun!

May 23rd

EXCITING SUPPORT

Here we go co-creator! I have a big smile on my face. Oh my God! Are you ready for the Law of Attraction story that is starting to unfold? Well, I just met with Sonia Choquette and interviewed her about her new book. I had hundreds of questions for her. I'm going to upload the video on YouTube right now. I was interviewing her about her latest book, *The Answer is Simple*. She is an amazing, amazing person. She was just so great to interview; so easy, flowing, and to the point. She was one of my favorite interview subjects. I just loved it.

What happened is that, at one point, I asked her how to become a bestselling author, which was somewhat inspired by her books because she writes about intuition. And you know what, co-creator? Oh my God, this is so juicy! I asked her how to become a bestselling author, and I added, *"Well actually Sonia, I don't know if you know, but I wrote a book."* So I gave her a copy of *I Lost My Job and I Liked It* while we were doing the video. She responded by saying, *"Why don't I interview you and introduce you as the book of the month on my website?"* Oh my, my, my! I'm going to be featured in Sonia Choquette's newsletter and on her website! She also just interviewed me about the book and she's going to upload that video on YouTube. I'm just overwhelmed by the amazing thing that just happened and how one thing led to the next.

FROM ONE MANIFESTATION TO ANOTHER

While I was doing my research before interviewing Sonia, I saw a video that she had made introducing Shamrock on YouTube, and I remember thinking, *"How cool would it be to interview him too?"* Well, he was actually with Sonia the day I interviewed her. I couldn't believe it. So, first I am interviewing Sonia, then I am interviewing Shamrock with Sonia and, after that, Shamrock is actually taking the video of Sonia interviewing me! Not only was Sonia generously providing me with tips on how to become a bestselling author, but she also gave me big kudos on the spot, and it's going to go out right now.

LET IT FLOW!

Co-creator, this is how the Law of Attraction works. It's not like strategy, you just let it flow. I'm so amazed! You have to check out the videos that I'm going to upload on YouTube very shortly, and you will see it for yourself. You can find them by searching on YouTube "Sonia Chochoquette Lilou Mace."

And even more cool, I just found out that Sonia is doing more and more flip camera videos and she told me she was inspired by my interviewing her that way back in Chicago over a year ago!

I'm just so amazed with the flow she shared with me during her interview.

SONIA'S QUICKIES TO SHIFT ENERGY

It's actually very interesting to interview Sonia. She was describing some tools and some quicken effects that can shift our energy. She also mentioned walking in nature, moving, singing, and breathing. She gave a number of different breathing exercises. I'll post all of those videos on the book's website because it is just fascinating to listen to her. It is inspiring to witness how when Life flows, things begin to happen so quickly. I look forward to reading Sonia's next book and interviewing her again. She really is amazing and is helping so many people.

SHARING AND PROMOTING INSPIRATION

I just love to share the inspiring messages of others and promote them. It is something I do spontaneously and lovingly. So it seems that the positive energy I have sent out is coming back to me. My mind couldn't have imagined Sonia Choquette being so generous and doing what she did for me. Wow. I feel like I am now vibrating at a bestselling author's frequency! Clearly, this was meant to happen during my really beautiful conversation with her. I feel that the Universe is sending the message that we still have choices and alternatives in this economy; in this climate. Instead of following our fears and anxieties, we must really follow our hearts. So many beautiful, beautiful, beautiful tips came from Sonia Choquette. What an honor.

PRE-CELEBRATION

When Sonia was flipping through my book, she came upon my memos on Veuve Cliquot champagne, pre-celebrating, and the memory of Daniel Moore. (Daniel is my best friend in the US. I would even say he is a soul mate. If you are reading these words Daniel, I love you). So Sonia made the comment, *'Veuve Cliquot is also my favorite champagne."* So, I'm on my way back following the interview and thinking, "*Maybe this is a good time to do a pre-celebration. Maybe I should get champagne and celebrate this moment?"* But it doesn't feel quite right yet.

So, I just stopped and got some really nurturing food. But my body felt like it needed meat, so I got some chicken that I will have with my lovely creamy avocados and some tomatoes. I also bought some roses. That's my pre-celebration; reminding me of my beauty, spirit, soul, and life. I got two little bouquets of roses, one for my desk and the other to put in the kitchen for my roommate Henrik, because I had promised him that I would bring flowers every week. Okay co-creators, speak to you soon. Time for lunch! Yum yum!

IT STARTS WITH A THOUGHT

It's interesting, thinking back to when I was getting ready to interview Sonia. I was thinking *"Well, I don't really need to look all pretty (with makeup) because I won't be in front of the camera."* But for some reason, I remember I had a quick change of thought that was just like, *"Well, maybe I'll need to look good, because... who knows?"* So I did my makeup, and I put on a nicer top. I did my hair. I was ready for what was about to manifest next.

So what may seem to be an insignificant shift in thinking can be very significant. Just like the brief thought I had of sitting next to Sonia and doing an interview; of being in front of the camera with her and introducing the question of how to be a bestselling author. I couldn't imagine that really happening, but I still had a brief thought about how it would feel if it did. In all honesty, I felt very hesitant about asking her that question because I didn't want to bother her with something that was not directly related to her own book. That is just the way I am. So I really had to step up and request help, which is what Sonia recommends.

REQUESTING HELP

At one point she said, "Lilou, you know all the authors that you're interviewing? You have got to ask them for their endorsement (of your book); ask that they interview you and ask them to put you on their websites." So there is a lot to be said about requesting help. I had never actually thought of doing such a thing because I worried that I would be bothering people. But Sonia definitely showed me the way. She is a bestselling author, and she gave me the same recommendation, co-creator.

A MISSION

I feel I have a mission! That mission is unfolding right now. I always knew it would. I always had that burning desire. But now as I advance into really daring to declare what I want to attract in my life, I'm becoming more and more present to the fact that there is something big out there. I declared a long time ago that I wanted to empower millions, and now I feel the time has come for that to take place. Something big is about to happen; something fulfilling, something magnificent, something warm, something spiritual and very real. So I welcome it and I'm learning to accept all that is good. I am open to receiving. I'm seeing that receiving is a bigger deal than I would have thought as it means allowing and opening up.

THINKING BIG AND BEING GRATEFUL IN THE NOW

My mom always tells me that I am never satisfied. But I think, somehow, that is what allows me to always welcome more and not be in a state of "whatever happens."

It's always important to find the right balance and make sure you are at the right level and grateful. I think gratitude is really, really key. I've always practiced being grateful, even more so over the past few years as I've applied the Law of Attraction. As I declare goals, I am grateful for every single little step that unfolds according to my declarations. I am grateful for all that is in alignment with my ultimate goal. Whether it is my 100-Day Reality Challenge intention or a segment intention, or whatever you want to call it. I'm grateful to be where I am right now. I'm grateful for all the wonderful people I'm meeting. I'm grateful for being in this space. I'm allowing myself to receive and to continue following my inner guidance.

May 25th

COMPUTER CHALLENGES

My computer would not start. I've been having little problems with it since I met with Sonia. I thought it was related to some video that I had uploaded. But my computer just doesn't want to start, and I am very pissed off at myself because I didn't back it up. And of course, in the computer are all the photos and videos that I have been recording recently including the video I did today. Everything is in the computer including the first 100 memos for this book. But, I've decided to still continue recording the memos.

I had a meeting scheduled today with my friend David King. We used to work together at Great Hotels, so I still went to meet with him. We were talking about the Law of Attraction and other things related to my previous work. And there was really an inspiring moment when I thought, *"You know what? You've got to do what you've got to do, and I'm still continuing this. So I'm focusing on the outcome. If it's happening, it's for a reason. I'm not going to dwell too much on this whole thing."* Maybe I was not supposed to start the book at this stage? Maybe it just wasn't supposed to happen for some reason? But I will make it happen, and I declare I will recover that data so that I can move forward with this.

May 26th

I just dropped off my iMac, and I'm now waiting to hear back about whether they were able to retrieve my data. I am sending positive energy. I'm breathing deeply in and out, in and out to calm my body and recenter myself. I also just did a little list of things that I'm grateful for as I'm walking around the neighborhood.

May 27th

AN OPPORTUNITY TO CONNECT IN PERSON

I just did a video about malfunctioning electronics because I think it happens to quite a lot of us as we are increasing our energy and vibration. In fact, I've seen a few blogs here and there covering the topic. So I did a video about it today; I'm uploading it right now. Since my computer is not working and is in the repair shop at the moment, I'm going to the Blackwell bookstore on Kings Crossroad. I believe I should take this opportunity to connect in person and go around to a few bookstores in the area.

The print-on-demand (POD) machine where my book was first printed is in the Blackwell book store. I'm going to bring a few copies of my book to another bookstore. We had all gotten together when I first came back to the UK from the US and stopped in this really cute self-help, spiritual bookstore. So I'm going to bring two copies of my books there and also bring two more or whatever I have left to Blackwell. I'll keep one extra copy just in case.

SUPPORT ALL THE WAY FROM AUSTRALIA

I just saw the wonderful video that Megan posted on YouTube where she's describing receiving my book. She's really sweet!

COMPUTER BLESSING TO CONNECT AGAIN

Before I ramble on too much, I'm off to some new adventures. I'm taking this opportunity to move beyond the computer and connect again. I really want to do more and more of this sort of thing. I want to start moving my body more; get back into the exercise. I've been running and practicing for the half marathon, but I have put on some weight. I know that I will just naturally get rid of it as I move more.

I'm also asking for signs from the Divine. I'm asking for guidance as to which bookstore I should bring my book and where I should be doing my book signing. All of it is happening, and it will be wonderful. It is very, very exciting!

I'm now in Leicester Square on my way to the bookstore. It is so easy to be obsessed about the goal, but it is also important to step back because I know it is going to happen. It is not my job to put intensity and focus on the outcome. I am thinking to myself, *"Yes, I want this. Yes, I want this."* But that is not how it is supposed to feel. I need to step back and know that everything is unfolding as it should. I need to detach myself, so that is what I am doing right now. I am reminding myself to do that. That's all for now.

SOME UPLIFTING NEWS

Good news, co-creator. The Apple Store was able to save the entire book file on my computer! It took a long time, but they have recovered it. So the book is moving forward. I am so happy. Yes! And now I just saw a copy of my book at the Blackwell bookstore in London. It is a big, big bookstore. I didn't realize how big it is!

We are considering doing the launch on Thursday, the 11th of

June from 7:00 pm to 8:00 pm at this bookstore. I can organize a party somewhere immediately following the book launch, but I'm really excited that the manager, Marcus, also suggested having wine and cheese at the actual event. There would be a whole area of the bookstore devoted to the book launch, so I could promote the book and bring in a lot of people. He thinks a group of 50 would be great.

CHAPTER 2: NO MONEY IN MY ACCOUNT

June 1st

SHOCKING NEWS

It is 11:00 am. My debit card was acting strangely the past two days. I wanted to take out some money, like £50 ($80). So I went to the HSBC branch on High Street Kensington. When I asked for the money, the bank clerk said, *"There is no money in your account, Ms. Macé."* I live in London. Life is very expensive here. I am quite shocked. This was unexpected.

Yet I know all this is happening for a reason. While I am focusing on making my book a bestseller, pursuing my dream job and aiming to empower millions of people in the process, I am faced with a "no money" situation. How embarrassing.

In the time since I lost my job on February 16th, I've been able to create a book, finance the book, and self-publish it in less than two months. I have also been paid for some of the author interviews I've done, which has enabled me to live a comfortable life and continue paying my bills. But now it is June 1st...and I have no money in my account.

NOT GIVING UP ON DREAMS

To say the least, I am not proud to be making this statement. In fact, I am totally ashamed. How could I have let this happen to me? What should I do now? Should I just get another routine job like I have had in the past? I know that this is not a coincidence. I have been wanting to write a book and have it become a bestseller. So I believe there is something important that I am supposed to understand (break through) right now. There is something I am meant to understand about what has happened so I can view not having money from a different angle. One thing I am clear about is that I don't want this to be an excuse for not making my dreams come true. I am not giving up.

I LOST MY MONEY AND I LIKED IT?

Yes, I have tears in my eyes right now. It's quite emotional. But there are still so many things for which to be grateful.

I live in London. I have found what I want to do with my life. I am living my dream job as a result of writing and publishing my first book (And if you still haven't figured out what your dream job is, you might consider reading it). Now, I am in the process of writing my second book and I wonder, is that book going to be called *I Lost My Money and I Liked It*? My thoughts are going back over recent events. Last week the hard drive in my new iMac (which I bought in March shortly after I lost my job) crashed, so I lost the data. I paid someone at the Apple Store quite a bit of money to recover the data. It is money that would have come in handy now.

NO IDEA WHAT'S NEXT

I have no idea what is coming next, co-creator. I am asking for the support of the Universe. I am asking for guidance. I'm simply allowing this to unfold because I believe that, out of this, something powerful can happen. I'm actually viewing it as a turning point because I don't want this problem anymore. I don't want to struggle to pay the bills. I don't want to struggle making ends meet. I don't want to be in this situation. So, even at this moment, I'm comfortable, because I know this situation doesn't define who I am. I know there is so much more to life once you have both love and money. And actually, just me saying the word "love" before saying the word "money," I feel something shift. I have a feeling that there's a correlation between the two. Yeah, it's about letting it go and letting something better come in. I've heard this many times. At least I believe this is true of authentic love and authentic money, if there is such a thing?

HOW CAN I ATTRACT MONEY NOW?

So now, co-creator, I am going to deal with this reality and ask for guidance. I'm going to write down different ways I can attract money. One good thing is that I have already ordered and paid for another box of 57 books, which is going to be delivered either today or tomorrow. I do have to admit that part of me has been resistant and shy about pursuing things, such as setting up seminars and book signings, or selling the books myself by going in person to different stores. So, maybe doing those things were all part of the process that was meant to unfold and, had I taken them on, I would not have found myself in this present situation.

THE BEGINNING OF SOMETHING BIG!

I don't want to waste any more precious time being angry at what's happening right now or being angry at myself because of my present situation. There is a huge opportunity for something better. I know this. When I woke up, I had a feeling it was going to be an awesome day and an awesome week. That is what I'm going for. Actually, if I'm being totally honest, I thought today was going to be a prosperous day, until I learned about my empty bank account. It may still be a prosperous day, because I am tapping into my own power, creativity, and abundance; the true wealth that exists inside of me. So today, June 1st, is actually the beginning of something big!

A PROSPEROUS DAY, A PROSPEROUS SEASON

I just received the boxes containing the 57 copies of my book, and my book is now also available for sale on Amazon.com and Amazon.co.uk. However, I will not receive the royalties from online sales until much later on. So as much as I need the book to get media attention right now, I have to think about both long-term and short-term income. So, this means that I do need to bring in some money right now. I need to find ways that are going to bring money in abundantly and make my book a bestseller. It's funny because I am in Season 12 of the 100-Day Reality Challenge, and my goal this time has been to attract love and money; to allow love and money to flow in. I wanted it to be a prosperous season.

FEELING NUMB

So now this is happening. I have no money in my account. I have to dig inside of me and let things happen, and I'm also going to write a journal. But I have to say right now that my mood is quite negative. There is so much that I need to do, but something within me is feeling very confronted. I know that I have to learn how to prioritize, but at the moment, I simply feel numb. I want to wake up, but part of me just wants to give up. Yet there is another part of me that is strongly anchored in wanting to make all the right things happen…and knowing that they can happen.

DEALING WITH RISING EMOTIONS AND FEARS

There are a couple of things that I'm listing in my journal of things that I can do. For example, through the 100-Day Reality Challenge, some copies of my books were purchased so a bit of money will be coming in. Also, Pat Daly, a client of mine in the US, will be sending me a payment that is due. I can sell the

57 books that I have in my possession, some by bringing copies to bookstores here in London. It is also important that I begin working on a marketing plan for the book so I can better prioritize what needs to be done.

RUNNING MY MIND

I am thinking of calling Baptist. Actually, calling Baptist would be a good thing to do. All the previous actions that I have listed are important, but, how can I say this? Those actions alone are not enough. Something else must be done; something that will allow abundance to flow into my life. I don't just want to put a temporary band aid on the problem. I need a long-term solution. So right now, I must breathe deeply in and out to relax my body and try to calm my mind...which is running, running, running.

TAPPING INTO THE REAL POWER

Part of me is angry over how I got to this point. I feel like I am in a deep hole, and I do not know who I can tell about this. It's not fair to tell my friends or even my flat mates. I'm just not ready for that. If I tell my mom, she will just get worried. My dad would probably react the same way. Of course, if I contacted my parents, they could send some money, but that is not going to help me tap into my own power—the real power and abundance that I know exists inside. So there are some actions that I must take right now that I might otherwise not have taken, and I have to prioritize those actions.

CLEANSING TIME

Now I'm going to cleanse. I had already decided to do a master cleanse when I was going to HSBC bank this morning to get a new card. Actually, I had stopped at the bank on my way to Whole Foods to get the maple syrup that I needed. I'm going to do this master cleanse for three days. There are a few good things about doing this now. First, it will clean my body. Second, it will clear my mind. And lastly, it will enable me to nourish myself at a very low cost. I think it is appropriate to do it right now while I am working on all the other issues before me.

WANTING TO HIDE

I'm going to check my US bank account, which may be able to help me a bit. There's not much in there either, but that's not the real issue. My bank account in the UK is empty. How can I use the Law of Attraction to help me?

I feel like praying right now; asking for help and guidance. I could spend some time in the park, or go for a run. But to be honest, I would just like to go under the covers and hide. I want to numb myself. I do not want to feel the disappointment, the pain, the guilt, the sadness, and the shame that my present situation represents.

FINDING RELIEF

Now I know that if I want The Law of Attraction to work in my favor, I need to focus on what I'm grateful for right now and what I do have to increase my vibration.

I'm definitely grateful for having an apartment. I'm grateful that most of my bills for this month are paid. I'm grateful that I received a full box of books that I can sell because the first box of books I literally gave away for promotion. Even now, part of me just wants to give away more copies of the book. It would be fun to just take one of these boxes and go to High Street Kensington and give them away, but I know that I need to sell them. I need to be strategic about what I do. I am organizing a book signing at Blackwell on June 11th, and I will have the opportunity to sell copies of the book at that event.

ASKING FOR HIGHER GUIDANCE

Actually, there's a friend I can reach out to...Chantal. I'm going to contact her to see if she is available to do a tarot reading for me because I know that would help. On the other hand, I know that we are the co-creators of our lives, and it is up to us to co-create our own reality. So going outside for a walk is probably what I need because I'm not being very productive about uploading anything online. Co-creator, I'm not sure what to do right now so

I am asking for Higher Guidance.

GOING FOR A WALK

Part of me is scared but another part of me is laughing at this. All I do know is that this is a moment that I can use to tap in and focus. As Sonia Choquette says, when you're in a bad vibe, just grab your keys and the sound of the keys in your hand will immediately put you in a different state of mind. So, even though I just want to crawl under the covers and hide, I'm grabbing my keys right now and I'm going for a walk.

1:11 pm: I am following Sonia Choquette's recommendation to shift my mood and move beyond negativity. Right now, I'm still dragging my feet, but as I was thinking about where to go, I decided that I would just go with the flow and see where my walk takes me. As I am walking, the thought comes to me that maybe I should go towards Fullham Road where I can drop off a book at an independent bookseller.

In all honesty, part of me is a bit worried about just showing up at a bookshop with a copy of my book, because I don't really need a rejection right now, but I also know that I should not be feeling so yucky and sad. I have many things to be grateful for. I have written a book. I am healthy. But right now, I am really dragging my feet.

ALLOW EVENTS TO UNFOLD

Anyway, I'm on my way towards Fullham Road. I can't even remember where that bookstore is, so I'm just going to keep walking and going with the flow. I know it is not very conventional to stop focusing on my current problem and take a walk instead, but I also know that sometimes this is how the most amazing things happen. So my goal right now is to simply allow events to unfold and the answers I need to manifest by opening myself up to new ideas and new people. I just have to relax and step back knowing that there are no coincidences in life and that all is happening just as it was meant to happen.

WHY GO ANYWHERE ELSE?

This weekend, I was at Mariana and Sean's wedding on the Southern coast of the UK. Mariana has been a member of the 100-Day Reality Challenge for the past two years, and she has just married her soul mate. It was really beautiful. I stayed over on Sunday and was hanging out at the beach. My friend Paul came and joined me because he also wanted to get a break from London and enjoy the beach. So why go anywhere else? London has been amazing.

AM I INCLUDING MYSELF?

Some spiritual teachers say that you have to give away what you want to receive in your life. I feel that I have been doing this. To be honest, I have recently given away so much of what I have wanted. I have been generous with both my work and with money. I've given nice presents to friends. I've interviewed authors and helped them promote their work without charging. My main intention is to share information that will inspire millions of people and attract true financial abundance into my life. So I'm not holding back on promoting people...except, maybe myself. Hmmm.

FEELING TRAPPED

Maybe I am doing all those wonderful things for others instead of doing them for myself? Maybe I am focusing on the success of others as a way to escape from the task of fulfilling my own dreams? These possibilities are something I must look at. I am asking for Higher Guidance and support. I'm willing to look at it now. I really feel trapped.

SELLING MY BELONGINGS?

The thought has crossed my mind to sell some of my personal belongings to get money. But I'm not going to sell anything that has great meaning to me. For example, I could be selling the beautiful watch with some diamonds that my friend Daniel gave me. But no, I cannot do that. Every time I wear the watch, it reminds me of Daniel and brings back memories that are precious to my heart. So I don't want to sell any of my belongings. I don't think doing that is the right answer to my problem anyway. Instead, I think it is time to pray, to tap into my own power, to reflect, and to step back. Right now, I'm just walking and hoping that I am heading in the direction of the bookstore. I have no idea. Gosh, it's warm in London. The heat is on!

WHAT IS THE NEXT INSPIRED ACTION?

It's amazing how difficult it can be to just let go. I could have just gone for a walk. Instead, I had to take three of my books with me thinking that maybe I would find a bookstore that will accept them. But is that going to fill up my bank account? I don't know. What is my next inspired action?

FINDING FREEDOM FROM HAVING NO MONEY

I have to say, although it is somewhat depressing, it is also liberating to not have to deal with money. I see HSBC bank right on the corner. There's a certain sense of freedom in not having that money! How about that!

June 2nd

FOLLOWING THE GUIDANCE ONE STEP AT A TIME

Oh my voice! I've got a cold. I'm on my way to Covent Garden where I spotted a couple of self-help bookstores that I would like to speak to about carrying *I Lost My Job and I Liked It,* so I took some books with me which I can potentially drop off. I'm just following the next inspiring steps. I'm not sure where I'm heading, but I know where I want to go. I'm not sure how I will get there, but that's none of my business as the Universe is taking care of that. The Law of Attraction is at work, it always is, and as I think and focus on what I want, I will attract it. And what I want is to inspire millions and make millions.

FROM BOOKSTORE TO BOOKSTORE

My account is now in overdraft! What an awful feeling I get from it. I feel stuck.

It is about 12:35 pm, and I just got out of Mysteries — a bookstore that is located on Monmouth Street 11, around the Covent Garden area. At the store, I met Kenny and she was so nice. I told her about my book and... (Sorry, I've got tears in my eyes, so I'm having quite a hard time recording this memo.) When she saw the book, I told her that I self-published it and that it was about the Law of Attraction. So she asked me if I wanted to have it handled by a publisher, and I told her that I was not considering that at first, but I now realize that it is something I need to do, because I'm having a hard time handling it on my own.

HOPE FROM MEN, MONEY AND CHOCOLATE

It took quite a lot to continue speaking with Kenny because I became emotional in front of her. But then she said, "Well there's this woman that wrote Men, Money and Chocolate. It's a novel, but it was actually bought by Hay House. That woman just sent in her manuscript and Hay House bought it and now she's doing great."

It gave me hope when I heard what Kenny had to say. Then, when she saw the Law of Attraction as part of the title of my book, she said, *"Well this is definitely something hot right now and I would love to have it."* So I told her I could leave one copy with her and then she said, *"Sure, but I would like more of them."* I had three additional copies with me and she took all three! I asked her to please give me a call if she started seeing that the book was selling, and I would be happy to ask for more copies.

So I'm officially in a bookstore that really wants me there. That's it for my morning adventure. Now I'm going to head back home because I feel quite weak from having a cold. I'm also doing the master cleanse, and it is unusually hot here in London. So, okay, that's my great news. I'm very thankful for this right now. Very thankful.

CREDIT CARDS ARE NOT REAL MONEY

I just want to clarify something here about credit cards because I had an experience with them back in the US. I lived in the US for nearly eight years and, as you know, it is tempting to use a credit card when you have one. You use it, you spend more than you earn, and you get into debt. That is not what I'm attempting here. I'm not going for credit cards. I'm not going for loans or anything like that. I'm purely using the abundance that I can attract by tapping into the real power. Getting into more debt would not help here. So, I'm not going that route. It will not help me fulfill my dream or tap into the potential for abundance that I know exists. I think money in general is just an excuse, but right now, I am not making any excuses. I am moving forward. But I wanted to point out that the card I was referring to earlier has just arrived and, it is a regular debit card, check card, *not* a credit card. Obviously, I'm not able to use it at this point, but I'm setting everything up to prepare for the abundance that I know is coming. Part of that preparation includes setting up a business account with HSBC.

NOTICING THE LOW SELF WORTH VOICES

I'm writing an email to a magazine in Germany, and I'm noticing that I was consciously shifting my energy while writing that email. That was because I finally heard the voice that was running through my mind. Recently, each time I have been sending email requests to magazines and newspapers asking them to write about my book, there has been this other conversation in the back of my mind that was saying, *"Yeah right. You're not worth it,"* and *"Who cares about your book and your story?"* and this is what has been running the show. That is the intent of the voice and the thoughts behind it. So even as I am writing, *"Oh please feature me,"* the negative voice is sending the thought, *"Oh no, they never will."*

IT STARTS WITH ME

So I'm finally coming to the realization that it has to start with me. It has to start with me believing that this is great stuff, because it is. It's just so stupid and silly to think any other way. I'm not going to simply dismiss those other thoughts. Instead, I'm going to embrace and nurture myself and my thoughts so that I'm thinking positively; so that I'm thinking that, yes, I am worth being featured in magazines. I have a message to get out, and so I'm going to shift my energy from now on. Each time I send an email, I will have an even more powerful intent. I have a deep knowing that I am worth it and that they will want to feature me. I know that they are asking for the exact type of story that I am offering and that they've attracted me instead of feeling like I am forcing myself on them or anything like that. So yeah, that's pretty cool.

MOVING AWAY FROM FEAR AND LACK

Okay, I'm beginning to see how things are starting to move forward when my focus is on success rather than on fear and lack. One example is that I just received confirmation from Blackwell bookstore that my book signing will happen on June 11th from 7:00 pm until 8:00 pm. So I'm now posting an invitation on Facebook and on "A Small World." I can start promoting the book signing, and we'll have wine and cheese at the event. I'll get people together. I'm really excited about that. I was able to post my first video on Intent.com as well to introduce myself to the community.

I've also received an email from Martha from WAYN. WAYN is a network of 13 million travelers around the world. WAYN stands for: "Where Are You Now?" and it was co-founded by Jerome, who has been of great support. They are putting together a special profile for me. I helped them promote one of their events, so now they are going to feature my book in a couple of weeks. I just received an email from Martha saying that they are moving things forward. So that's great as I look forward to all the support I can get.

June 5th

NEW YORK TIMES BEST SELLERS

I'm on the New York Times website looking at their criteria for a book to become a bestseller on their list. On their website it says: "Rankings reflect sales at almost 4,000 bookstores plus wholesalers serving 50,000 other retailers, gift shops, department stores, newsstands, supermarkets statistically weighted to represent all such outlets nationwide."

Oh, I'm not in bookstores, so I feel quite down by that news. I have to ask myself if it is really the status of being a *New York Times* bestselling author that I want or if it is selling millions of copies of my book and empowering people? And I think it's really about empowering people, making money, and allowing prosperity in all forms to come in. It's not so much about being a *New York Times* bestseller, which is a numbers game and a status game, but shouldn't be an end in itself. So I'm going to do a bit of visualization to recenter myself, to focus, to take the time to step back and ground myself. I am going to breathe deeply in and out and allow some new ideas to flow.

A GREAT MAN HAS LEFT THIS PLANET TODAY

I just heard the devastating news yesterday evening that Hank, a very dear friend of mine who lived in Michigan and who I mention in *I Lost My Job and I Liked It,* has died at the age of 68 years old. He had a terrible heart attack. His son sent me an email with the news. Apparently, Hank died instantly and there was no pain. I'm shocked and very sad. I cannot quite believe it. I know that the spirit prevails and he's around all the time now, but it's so hard to take it all in. I am asking, why him and why now? He definitely lived a full life. He was someone who knew how to have both great laughter and great success in his life. Right now, I am thinking of his family and the dog he loved so much and how his pet must also be really, really sad.

COMMUNICATING WITH HANK FROM THE OTHER SIDE

I'm starting to talk to Hank in a new way now and my first message to him is, "If you hear this, Hank, I send you much love. You are here in my heart and always will be. I love you dearly, and I wish I had had more time with you. I thank you for all the help you gave me; all your words of wisdom. You will always remain a powerful icon in my life."

I am also thinking that Hank did not have the time to publish his book. He told me that I had inspired him, and he wanted to write the story of his life. He was one of my great mentors. He was someone who I could always talk to so openly and freely. I could always be myself with Hank. I feel so alone right now. I hope Hank is doing well wherever he is. I am asking him to give me a sign, to be here with me in spirit, and to let me know how I can help him.

So, my dear friend Hank just passed away. A great man has left this planet.

EMERGING POSSIBILITY OF CREATING SOMETHING NEW

I just had a great conversation with my friend Cilou. I'm the godmother of her child, Sarah June, and it's always good to speak with her. It's funny how the people that I'm speaking to right now, are the same people in pretty much the same sequence that I was speaking to during the realization of my first book. And, to tell the truth, it feels like it's a whole new beginning; a huge step. I can now see that the book came together one small piece at a time with me putting the pieces together.

But now, when I step back and allow myself to be the observer of that reality, I see that I'm at the beginning of creating something new. So, of course, there will be ups and downs, drama and fear, moments of scarcity, and the richness of dreams. But right now,

I am experiencing a great mix of emotions, especially with the death of Hank.

Hank was always a great advisor, always available to answer my emails and any questions that I had. So I feel I've really lost a part of myself with his passing, and it is time for me to grow up. It is time for me to move forward in fully pursuing my dreams. I know that there is nothing that Hank would want me to do more.

LETTING PEOPLE IN

My conversation with Cilou was great and very nurturing. I told her what was going on; what was really happening with me. I want to be completely honest about this financial situation with my friends. In the past, I had some financial issues that I never really shared with them. But this time, I really need to let people in and let them know the truth. Now my family, especially my mom, is a different issue. I don't want her to worry, so I'm not going to go there at this point.

I'm looking for Higher Guidance so I can open myself up to new ideas, new possibilities, and a new way of thinking. Trying something new is really what's coming out of this experience. Trying new things, trying new ways of being; things that I wouldn't normally do. It is time for me to get out of my comfort zone so the creative flow I feel can get charged up.

PERSONALIZED COPIES

I'm on my way to the gym to get a good workout. I just sent an email to everyone saying that I would sign copies of *I Lost My Job and I Liked It* and ship it to them. I received an overwhelming number of responses, so that was encouraging. I posted a picture of the book and the reviews online and said, *"Get your copy today. I'll ship it, personalize it, and sign it for you."* The number of emails was amazing. So I feel very, very blessed. Money is coming in, co-creator!

We're really energy beings. Everything is energy. Money is energy. It's just a matter of tuning into that energy and relaxing.

LEWIS MADE MY DAY

I received an email from Lewis Pugh, an amazing leader and swimmer who swam across all the oceans and trains with Olympic teams. He told me that he is loving my book. He said, *"I've got so much work to do, but I just received your book in South Africa and I can't put it down."* Lewis is absolutely an amazing person. He really made my day by sharing those wonderful words with me. I thank him very much.

TAKING A STAND

I just stopped at the Borders Store, Border Express on Fulham Road, and I showed a clerk there my book and said, *"I want this book to be represented in your store because people need help right now dealing with job loss."* I have a big smile. The more I get the story out, the better.

BEING NUMBER ONE ON AMAZON

I received a new little message from Sonia Choquette that said she was number one for a few days on Amazon and, you know what? That's what I want! That's what I'm aiming for. Number One on Amazon sales for maybe a couple of days. Yeah, baby. That sounds juicy. Now that turns me on.

June 9th

WAKING UP WITH MORE NEGATIVE THOUGHTS

I woke up feeling so stressed and having dark thoughts. I am just not seeing anything ending up right, and I'm thinking of all the starving artists out there. I am feeling totally disillusioned and having thoughts of scarcity...and on and on. Why do I keep going up and down in my emotions? What a rollercoaster! When is this going to stop?

MEDITATION TO RELEASE FEARS

I decided to do a meditation with Doreen Virtue. It is a 30-minute meditation mainly based on releasing fears. I am feeling better, but I still have a way to go. Meditation definitely points out how important it is to have faith in your natural abilities. It helps you to focus on what you're good at, which is also your life purpose. This goes back to what I'm always hearing, which is if you trust with all your heart, then things can happen. But at times, this is such a hard process. I feel that part of me hasn't made the declaration powerfully enough to the Universe, so I really need to reaffirm it.

MY PRAYER TO THE UNIVERSE

I'm praying right now to the Universe. I cannot see anything else. I want to pray from the bottom of my heart: "Please help me to have faith in my abilities. Please give me strength, creativity, and ideas to align my spirit to Source. I know I'm a powerful co-creator. I just lost a bit of my faith right now, and I'm dwelling in the fear. Help me to remove that fear. Protect me. I am opening myself up to receive. Please send me your guiding angels to protect me. I'm opening myself up to the abundance of the Universe." (I breathe deeply in and out).

"God, I'm afraid right now. I'm confused and fearful. Am I deserving? Do I deserve this greatness? Can you help me allow it in? Can you help me open my heart again? Can you help me receive? I pray to you, God, today. As I'm kneeling, bowed on my bed, tears dropping on my face, I pray to you from the bottom of my soul. My heart is fully engaged. Help me to empower other people. Help me to help others. Help me to spread the message of this book to the media, to the public, everywhere. I need your support now."

"I'm creating the possibility, and I declare to the Universe, that I will receive the support, the guidance, the mentorship to reach my goals, to reach personal success, and that I won't see that as a destination but as a beginning for something even bigger and more transforming. I just want to see the journey. Please bring the abundance into my life, so I can bring abundance into the lives of others. Please help. Please. Help. I don't want my life to be a battle. I'm releasing. This is so hard, but fighting doesn't bring me anywhere except to worry. Being afraid doesn't lead me anywhere. So I surrender. I surrender."

Okay, that felt good. Apart from crying a lot right after I surrendered, I just took a deep breath. It was like my entire body filled with that breath. It was so deep. I have never taken a breath like that before. My mouth opened up wide and it was like my entire body just wanted to draw Life Force inside of me and fill up with it. I felt like I was energizing every single cell of my being, and I did it about 20 times; deep, deep, deep breathing. I don't know where that came from, but I do know that I feel at peace right now.

I AM NOT ALONE

I don't feel alone. I thank the Universe for the abundance it has already brought into my life. I thank the Universe for everything that I have in my life and I apologize for not always feeling satisfied with what I currently have. I understand that I'm very lucky right now. I know that I am blessed in this present moment.

So what's next, Universe? Show me the way. I am looking for your guidance, feeling your guidance. I am looking for the next inspired action. I am open to what feels right. Show me the way. I allow Life to flow through me. I want to be a servant of Life. Show me. Show me. Yes, show me. Show us all.

BOOK LAUNCH DATE

Okay, so I guess the Universe has decided that my book launch will take place on June 18th from 7:00 pm until 8:00 pm. I feel more comfortable with that as well. I also notified my friend Grant. He is managing the book launch party for me at the Kingly Club in London where he works. This is a trendy club with great music, and he has managed to accept RSVPs for up to one hundred people for a free cocktail and free entrance before 10:30 pm. So everything is set up now for June 18th, and I'm going to have more time to promote the party. That is absolutely wonderful. I feel abundant. Thank you.

J.K ROWLING WAS AS BROKE AS I AM

I remembered how J. K. Rowling took her Harry Potter story to an endless number of different publishers and was rejected time and again. At that point in her life, she had no money, but because she believed in the book she had written, she ultimately found a publisher who believed in her, and she became the richest woman in the UK. There is a meaningful lesson in her experience, and the tipping point that she had. I had forgotten about her story, and I hadn't realized how broke she had been before she achieved her dream. So I'm going to do some YouTube research and try to find some videos about her life.

STEPPING BACK AND HAVING FAITH AGAIN

It looks like I'm getting back in the flow again and remembering to allow the Universe to respond (deep breath). I'm just stepping back and having faith. I can see how each time we try to force events, it simply doesn't work. For example, I wanted the book launch to take place on June 11th because I love the number 11, so I pushed my publisher, Lightning Source, and I pushed the bookstore, Blackwell, to make it happen on that day. But it was not a natural process, and so it was not meant to happen. I could have asked to have the book launch on June 18th right up front, but I had decided *"the sooner the better"* so the Universe stepped in and I was given a lesson about how to step back and just allow events to unfold when they are meant to happen. So now the book launch will take place on June 18th. It is the date that the Universe has chosen.

PANACHE-FUL

The definition of panache: *"A grand or flamboyant manner. Verve, style, flair."* This is a word used in the status line of one of my Facebook friends. Her name is Sophy, and she lives in Australia. I have never met Sophy in person, but for some reason, I checked her status today and I just love that word panache. It has so much energy, so much greatness and so much passion in it. Here is how Wikipedia defines it:

"Panache is a word of French origin that carries the connotation of a flamboyant manner or reckless courage."

That is definitely an inspired word, isn't it? Panache. That really gets me thinking. I can see that it is a word that carries so much energy. I was inspired when I saw it. I can't even explain what it does to me but, hmmm. At the same time, it's got ambition, leadership, and energy attached to it. Panache is really juicy. It is a word that inspires me right now. So I'm going to have a panache-ful day!

A MIRROR TO YOUR LIFE AND EMOTIONS?

We're all on this personal journey. We all go through similar emotions and fears, don't we? That became even clearer to me through the feedback I got from my book. There are many mirrors in life. My story may mirror some of the things that you are doing, or could be doing, and by recognizing those similarities, in the end, it helps both of us to find our way to acceptance.

I'm a person that likes to wake up other souls. I like to wake people up to their reality and their potential. Yes, this is a more in-depth observation. But all the insights, the challenges, and the successes in my story are real. I'm not making any changes to what I share with you; how my experiences unfold. I want to keep my story real and authentic. There is true power in that.

We are all similar. We just look different. Each of us have unique skills, unique passions, and unique aspirations, but we want the same outcome. We want to be happy, to connect, to love, to be heard, to help, don't we?

KEEP DREAMING NO MATTER WHAT!

Oh, I love receiving all the messages from around the world! I just received an email from John Cappelli in which he says, *"Dreams. The dreams you have are yours, and if you believe and you really want them, then you put in effort."* He then attached a link to a video of *The Rookie*. *The Rookie* is a movie; I think it was actually a Walt Disney movie. And it's a great reminder that dreams are possible. I think we all need to be reminded of that. So I thank him very much. Let's keep dreaming no matter what!

June 11th

BACK IN THE FLOW

Things are flowing again. Just now, I received a message from Marla Martenson, and she says that she just got my book *I Lost My Job and I Liked It,* and she loved it. She's the author of *Excuse Me, Your Soul Mate is Waiting*. She asked me to send her the book cover, and she will be blasting it on her website and on her page called "Marla's Page." So that's really nice, and I'm going to send her the book cover right now.

Also, I had previously sent an email to my friend, Kevin Ross, who is the author of *The Designer's Life.* I interviewed him on *My Juicy Life* in Chicago. It was a TV show that I was producing and hosting, and he told me he was really excited about the book. I had originally contacted him for an interview, but he ended up calling me on Skype, and we were able to talk and catch up. I even saw his little girl. We were able to do a video chat and he said, *"Well Lilou, I want to interview you on my radio show on Unity FM..."* He apparently has around 19,000 listeners tuning in both online and over the radio. So he's going to interview me on his radio program. We set up a time on June 24th to do that, and I'm really enjoying this.

Right now, I'm going to get ready as some friends and I are going to do a girls' night out at Café Boheme in Soho and have fun.

June 12th

PRAYING MORE

I've been speaking more to God lately and praying. I just felt the need to hang on to something. I was raised Catholic, but I have also always felt deeply spiritual, understanding that there is something else outside of us, a force. But I have to say that when I was feeling really, really scared and hitting rock bottom (which I have shared with you) the only thing I felt I could do to bring myself a sense of hope, love, energy and support...was to pray.

I'm thinking about that right now because I just found myself praying to the image of Mary that I have in my wallet. It is something that one of my grand dads used to wear around his neck. It's a Virgin Mary, and I have it in my wallet. On one side, I can even see the wear from him holding it in his hand and touching it as he prayed. I can feel his energy, his strength, and his love through it, and that is what is with me right now.

FEELING ABUNDANT

I just thanked the Universe for enabling me to empower millions of people and for allowing me to be an agent of love, help, and service in this world. I feel ready. I feel really blessed to be able to share my journey at this moment. I am so grateful for everything. I don't have much in my bank account as yet, but I feel abundant in this present moment...as if that has already happened. I am so grateful that I have enough, to be able to ship my books, pay for my food and bills right now.

June 13th

LOVING MEN, MONEY AND CHOCOLATE

I just landed in France. The weather is absolutely amazing. The perfect temperature. Ah, it feels so good on the skin. I'm waiting for my mom to come and pick me up. I've been reading *Men, Money, and Chocolate* on the flight, and it's such a delight and joy. It is a novel, but it focuses on a spiritual quest that Maya, the main character, is living. It's actually a very insightful book that touches upon weight issues, finding men, and reaching success in life. The story in the book makes a great deal of sense and resonates with me. I must first make my personal dreams come true, before I can hope to attract the man of my dreams. That is important, because otherwise we search for someone to make us happy, when it is something we must do for ourselves.

So I do want to find success and find myself so I can be with somebody successful and have the perfect balance. So I'm going to focus on making this dream come true. Until I do that, I won't be totally present and available. I feel that moment is coming, and it is going to be great.

Men, Money, and Chocolate is a beautiful story. I don't think it's going to take me too long to finish reading it because it's such a good book, I can't put it down. I so look forward to meeting the book's author, Menna van Praag. She lives in Cambridge and while I'm reading her book, I'm thinking that it would be great to interview her.

100% COMMITED

I feel like I need to focus 100% on being financially free and making my dream come true before I can truly welcome my soul mate into my life. It was described so well in Menna's book. As long as you continue to seek your own happiness through another person, you cannot have a truly long-term, beautifully balanced relationship.

I've always focused on my career, but I've never been fully, 100% committed to it because a part of me has always thought, *"Oh yeah, but I can always be saved when the right man enters my* life," or *"This would be a great time to meet someone."* But now my mind has shifted, and my focus is 100% on writing this book. I am so, so eager to succeed here. I've never wanted it more. I really have a burning desire. It was not the same desire when I created the previous book. Back then it was to find my dream job. It's actually quite a powerful place to be. I feel so creative. I'm doing some deep breathing right now.

LOTTO IS NOT FOR ME

It's so interesting to me that some people play the Lotto, my mom included. She always plays Lotto. She's got a nice house, but she would love a new kitchen. There is a Lotto game that has been around for years, and playing it gives her hope. One day, maybe six months ago, I personally decided that playing the Lotto was not for me. I said, *"You know what? I'm not going to bother ever playing those kinds of games again because that is not how I want to make money."* I mean, frankly, there's nothing juicy about playing the Lotto. It sets up a distorted relationship with money. So many Lotto winners end up going back to the life they had before they won, if not a much worse situation, and it makes them miserable in the process. I'm just not going to attract money that way! I feel empowered; not waiting for it as a one day fantasy.

Yes, I want to be wealthy and help others. I will be making that money from projects I am involved in, something I have personally created, or something in which I have participated. That doesn't mean it cannot be large amounts of money. As for the people that win the Lotto, I think that's fantastic. I think that's great. I just have a different vision for attracting money. I feel Lotto is not my path in this lifetime. I would just create false hopes for myself. That does not serve me.

GIVING BACK TO MOM AND DAD

My mom has been generous to me. She made it possible for me to have a fantastic education and great opportunities in life. *"Thank you so much mom, for all the amazing gifts that you have given me. I want to give it back to you someday."*

And the same thing is true with my dad. I can't wait to give back to him. I want to get him clothes. Sometimes I know that he hesitates doing this for himself because he is thinking, *"No, I can't spend money on these clothes."* So I just want to spoil him with wonderful clothes because he is in such great shape for a man his age, and he will look so fantastic. Being able to do that for my dad will just be awesome; taking him shopping and saying, *"My treat!"* Oh, co-creator.

INVESTING IN OURSELVES

I think we should all invest more in ourselves and give ourselves a chance. I think we don't invest enough in our own success. I think we should all attend seminars, read books, go on retreats, buy informational DVDs and videos, and get massages. There are just so many amazing speakers out there and seminars that are mind blowing. I always get so much more from those experiences than I put in. Yeah, that rocks. That's juicy, juicy, juicy, juicy, juicy!

GROUNDING IN MEDITATION

I'm feeling so excited right now. I'm going to have to reground myself because my vibrations are quite high. I am thinking about what Deepak Chopra was saying earlier in his blog. He was describing how important meditation is because it is a place where you have access to your higher self. He made a good point. I know that meditation works. I've been doing meditation on and off. I think it was back during my 100-Day Reality Challenge either season five or six where, every morning, I did a 10-minute meditation. And let me tell you, it was mind blowing. It is a discipline at first, but I really want to start taking this on again and incorporate a little bit more each time, like visualization and deep breathing. I'm going to do that right now, actually.

PROMOTING A GREAT BOOK AND LIVING THE DREAM

I just uploaded this video telling my subscribers on YouTube about Menna van Praag's book. I just loved it, so I created a spontaneous video. I have the video featured on my page. I definitely want to help her, so I've tagged the video and also sent her a message. I also would love to interview her in person.

HIGH VIBRATIONS

I cannot even believe how creative and focused I am around money and wanting to make this happen. I'm obsessed! I love it! I'm having so much fun. My mind is completely focused on how I can make this happen, instead of wasting energy worrying about all the reasons why it's not possible. I'm totally focused on possibility. This is so magical. This is so juicy. I love this flow. Anything is possible in this flow. I'm totally in the zone. I should start meditating again. Boy, I'm vibrating high. I'm having a good laugh.

June 14th

RAISING THE BAR IN ALL AREAS

It is 10:00 am French time, and I just finished an hour run. The reason I'm bringing this up and sharing it in the book is because I'm a big believer in the need to raise the bar on all levels in our lives when we want to achieve success. Fitness is one of them. That's why I'm registered at the half marathon in Palma de Majorca, and now I'm at the stage where I'm running an hour, about ten kilometers. I committed to doing that today before picking up my grandma. I'm going to have a family day. I will have a good, healthy breakfast and enjoy the present moment with my family.

PRESENT TO THE MIRACLE OF LIFE

I'm on my way to get my 85-year-old grandma. She is such a delight. Driving right now toward Angers, and I'm just so present to the miracle of life and how life is beautiful if we allow it to be. I'm so grateful right now. I'm listening to a song on the radio. This song is just so magical and makes me feel so centered. This is the miracle of life. I know this might sound corny to some of you, but I cannot tell you often enough how grateful I am for this journey. I really, really get that everything that matters is in the journey, not only the destination.

BE, DO, HAVE

I've heard it many times but right now, I have to say the value of the process is so great. When you can align yourself with greatness, that's exactly what it takes to get there. You must vibrate success right now, already be in that state of mind, and have successful thoughts to be successful now. Whatever you want to call it, you need to be this *now* for it to come into your reality. It's not *"do, be, have."* It is *"be, do, have."* You have got to be in a successful mindset, then you will do successful things, and you will have success. It is a process that is simply unlimited.

There are so many people in this world that have created products and successfully done things in a unique way. When I am present to that reality, I'm like, *"Yeah, that could be me too."* When I was taking my shower earlier, I realized that I love marketing a product. I've always marketed services, and I was thinking, now I have a book. I love developing a product and then having a product to sell. It's brilliant. I really, really like it.

TAKING THE FIRST STEP

As you are reading this book, I encourage you to go to the very back where there is an area for notes. Just write down the ideas that pop into your mind as this journey is unfolding. Keep track of the things you want to remember and the actions that you are going to take on. It starts with a thought, but then it's the action that is going to generate whatever you want to generate.

That's one thing that I have always done. I already had a business in the US for eight years that I started when I was 24 years old after 9/11. Before that, I had been working for a tour operator in sales and marketing after I graduated. I moved to the US, then France, and then the UK; I have dual citizenship. Because of the events of 9/11, I lost all my commissions. I knew that I wanted more control over my finances, so I started my own business. At the time, I was living in Fort Lauderdale, Florida (I love that city), and I started an online marketing company. For the first six months until the moment where I was making enough with my own business, I worked as a waitress in the evenings to make some money. And my point here is that the most important thing is to get started; to be engaged in this process with passion.

Sometimes we can over-analyze. That is especially true in France where you have to be a certain way, and you need to do all the research and everything. While I think this is super important, I also think the main thing is to engage, take action, and get started. Whether it's to register a domain name, or to register the company; take the first step. As Martin Luther King, Jr. once said, *"Faith is taking the first step even when you don't see the whole staircase."*

FOLLOW YOUR HEART

You need to get started. If you feel strongly about something, and you're passionate about something, do it. I'm all about that. I really believe that we could all be self-employed. I know that some people prefer to work for other people. I really think when you want to reach a certain financial success, you do need to partner; you need to create your business. We all have unique skills and talents and, most of all, we should really focus on what we love because that is what we're good at. And that's my point here. If you focus on something that you're good at, that is where you will find your heart.

When I started a TV show in Chicago, I was producing it, hosting it, and yet I had no idea what I was doing. I had never done that before, but I followed my heart. Now I'm in the process of making my dreams come true, and it's giving me some juice. I love interviewing people, but back then, it was totally crazy to think that I could do that. Yet there was something about it that I just loved and wanted to do, so I did it. And I still love interviewing book authors; my dream is to one day have a national or even an international TV show. Then I will interview the world's most successful people and world leaders and, through my interviews, make that information available to many, many other people. That is a juicy vision, and it speaks to me!

LOVE WHAT YOU DO, LOVE YOUR JOB

We don't need to figure it all out, but at least if your heart is in whatever you do, you will enjoy doing it and be very good at it. And that is very, very important these days because there is so much competition for jobs in this economy. Frankly, it's so much more fun when you love what you're doing. You transcend challenges. You put your heart into it and, yes, there is a risk of getting hurt, but isn't it worth it? If that should happen, you learn from it and then you move on. I guess it's the same with love. But you see, I'm more reluctant when it comes to love. But it's good that I'm arriving at this conclusion about business because I can see that I already know how to take a risk with love because I have put myself so many times in the position of risking failure. For example, look at a child. When they first start walking, they fall again and again but then one day they can walk! Yeah! Well, that is because they have made a really strong commitment to walking. They just want to walk! They want to do what others are doing. They want to be free. They want to be able to get around and travel greater distances. But whatever the motivation is, failure is not the issue. The issue is your desire to keep going and that is how we should be in life. I don't think we risk enough.

STEPPING OUTSIDE OF THE COMFORT ZONE

We each have to step outside of our comfort zone. As long as you stay in your comfort zone, nothing juicy is going to happen. The juiciness, the vitamin of life, the amazing current, the passion, the surprises, and the miracles all require stepping outside of our comfort zone. You're never going to get all that in status quo because status quo is predictable. It's boring.

Yes, going beyond our comfort zone is challenging. You don't know what you're going to get. You feel uncertain, uneasy, but it's something new that you're discovering. It's like being on a new planet. It's like going to another country. It's like getting out of your comfort zone constantly. It could be talking to a stranger. It could be organizing a seminar, or planning a party, or talking to that new person, or picking up that phone. Ask someone you admire to become your mentor. Register your company. Quit your

job. Go talk to that person that you like. Get out of the box! Get –
Out – Of – The – Box and be committed to living life fully.

BRING IT ON!

Take the 100-Day Reality Challenge for crying out loud. You can
join us at www.cocreatingyourreality.com. Set a goal for 100 days
to live a life of passion and purpose, to live a juicy life, to attract
success, to step out of that comfort zone. Be part of a community
of like-minded people who will support you in your goals for one
season. Set those goals, blog and video blog, and watch your
life. *Watch your life*. Yes, you'll be confronted. Yes, you'll be
challenged, and that's a good thing. Without those experiences,
you won't learn the lessons that will bring you to a whole new
level. Yes, co-creator, I'm very passionate about this subject. I
am. I can't tell you enough how good this feels! Regardless of
the amount of money that I have in my bank account, I'm really
getting that this is not defining who I am right now, and I'm happy.
Why? Because I'm going for it. That's the juice! That's the juice!

MY HEART HAS BEEN CLOSED

I'm so amazed about the power of the heart, and I'm really
becoming very present to it because my heart was closed for
so long. Part of this was because of my parents divorcing. I was
deeply hurt by that and closed my heart, and then I never wanted
to open it again. But recently, I've been working on reopening

my heart. I reconciled with my dad fully. We had an amazing conversation a month or two ago while doing a river cruise in Amsterdam. During that cruise, we fully bonded and said some things to each other that really needed to be said. We spoke of how much love we have for each other. I think that really helped both of us to heal a lot of things.

I also noticed recently, with all the amazing books I've read and the authors I have interviewed, that everything seems to be about love.

LOVE KEEPS SHOWING UP

So, although I am working on prosperity, at the same time love keeps showing up. The more I open my heart and let go, the more I'm present to the abundance of this planet. The more I'm letting in love from other people, the more I'm allowing myself to receive on so many levels. For example, right now I'm going through all the messages that were sent to me through Co-Creating Our Reality, the community I co-founded. I began replying to everyone, and I became present to how much love exists there.

I really have to thank Sonia Choquette. Sonia is writing a book that will be out in 2010 called, *Traveling at the Speed of Love*. Things like that keep on showing up and feeding my soul right now because I'm opening myself up to them, and it's absolutely juicy. I'm very grateful because it feels good to let all of this in. So it is my intention to open my heart more each day. I feel it is really open right now, and I want to share it with the world. It feels so good and I feel so alive. I've been so scared to do this, but now that my heart is opening up again, it's just beautiful.

OPRAH WINFREY AND *THE COLOR PURPLE*'S INSPIRATION

Funny how every time I look at my clock it is 11:00, or some other combination of the number 11. I take that as a sign that I'm on track. That works.

I just came back from the post office, and I was thinking about an Oprah Winfrey story. There was the time when she was obsessed about being in the movie *The Color Purple*. She wanted a role in that movie so much and had done everything she could think of to get it. At the time she weighed over 200 pounds, so she decided she would just go to a fat farm (as she called it) to lose weight. Again, this was in the hope of getting a role in the movie. Once at the fat farm, she recalled singing out something like, *"I surrender. I surrender all."*

Once she finally released all her obsession, she received a phone call from Steven Spielberg, the director of *The Color Purple*, asking for her and saying, *"Don't lose any weight. We want you in The Color Purple to play Sophia"*.

I'm remembering this right now because Oprah is definitely a person that I admire. I met her four times in Chicago. She really is the one that sparked me to follow my dreams.

LET IT DO THE WORK

Sometimes it can be a difficult thing, when we really, really want something. It's important to have this burning desire, this eagerness, and to just want to make it happen. But the problem is, when you become too obsessed with something, you have too tight a grip on it, and you're not letting it go so the Universe can do its part. You are not having faith. Instead, you are sending the message that you don't really believe what you most want is going to happen.

I know I cannot generate the best ideas while I am being obsessive. That's the logical aspect. The spiritual aspect is that you have to let the Universe do its work. From whatever angle you want to look at this, what we need to do is release our hold on things. For me, that means going for a run, or even just a walk. When I find myself having obsessive thoughts, I'll go for a walk. Getting out in nature may not give me the answer, but it helps me see things differently right now.

YOU ARE NOT THE ONLY ONE WANTING TO SUCCEED

This afternoon, Guy, my mom's partner, told me: *"There is more than one person that wants to succeed."* That hurt me. I wish he was more supportive and uplifting. He made that remark after I shared with him how much I want success, and he basically told me, *"Well, you're not the only one."* And I get that. I really get that. And it's really a fantastic thing because every person wanting success is still going forward in spite of the challenges. Every person is still continuing and pursuing success by tapping into this energy. So we're all here together moving forward. We're not in competition. We are not giving up. We are continuing. We are in different industries, all kinds of businesses, and we are *helping* each other. We live in absolutely amazing times.

Anyway, co-creator, I'm going to get back in the sun for a little bit and enjoy the end of the day before I do more work. It's already 7:20 pm, but the sun is shining beautifully here in France.

OPENING UP TO RECEIVING FURTHER HELP

I have become very present to the support I am getting. I was already receiving support, but now I'm really grateful for and present to that support. That's what is so beautiful about making declarations and getting it out there, or, as I like to call it, *daring to declare* what you really want. It's like you're ready, you say it, and then it happens. That makes you even *more* present to it and, therefore, creates even more.

Abundance is showing up. There's timing for everything, and I'm very grateful right now, and I'm opening myself up to receiving help. I am declaring to the Universe:

Please send me support. Send me people who want to help spread this news; people who believe in this book and its message. Allow them to help me get this message across.

I release this book to the Universe. I put it in your hands so it will reach the right people, touch their hearts, and we can get the message out that this is a time for change. This is a time for a new evolution. This is a time to go for our purposes and help each other. Allow my message to go through. Give me the support from all the people wanting to help. I'm opening myself up to receive help and support in a big way. I thank you very much in advance. I am greatly appreciative of all the support right now.

June 17th

LESSON FROM A NEAR DEATH EXPERIENCE

It is a beautiful sunny day in France. I'm flying back to London today. Last night I was listening to an interview with Mellen-Thomas Benedict. It was an absolutely fascinating story. Mellen had a near-death-experience that he can recall in great detail. He was saying how much that experience changed his life. During his NDE, he was shown his life in review and he realized that his heart wasn't open to all the people who had tried to love him and help him. He didn't have faith in the goodness of human beings. He just wasn't there.

Listening to his fascinating story reminded me how the only thing that is really important is being in the present moment. Recently, I had some fears jump back in again, and I had to refocus my thoughts. I took a step back and said to myself, *"You know what? The only thing that really matters, the only thing that's real is now. The past is not. The future is not. So what can I do right now to make a difference? What can I do right now to feed a life? What can I do right now to get this message out?"* That's really where it's at. So I am reminding myself right now of the importance of living in the present moment.

TAKING OUR LEADERSHIP ROLES

Stores are closing. People are struggling. People are losing jobs. Some people don't even have enough to have proper nutritious food. While, at the same time, other people are asking for pay raises because they are not content with what they have. What kind of world do we live in, co-creator?

 We need to step up as leaders on this planet. I invite you to do so now. People must create products and services that are going to help this world become a better place. Each and every one of us must see that we have a responsibility. We can help. This is the time to shine, to get it all out. Now that I have both my feet firmly grounded in reality as I never had before, I want to really give it all I have now. Oh yes, I am.

MY WHOLE WORLD HAS COLLAPSED

My mom just dropped me at the airport in Nantes to get my plane to London. Along the way, there was crying and screaming. It turned into quite a drama. Now I'm not only cross with my dad (I had a big argument with him yesterday) but with my mom as well, and I am crying at the airport on my way to London. I feel like my whole world has collapsed. I feel like a little girl that isn't loved by her parents.

But on the other hand, I really think that it's time for me to face myself. This is not a time to find love. This is not a time to play around. This is a time to confront reality and make things happen with no excuses. There is no backup plan possible. I'm on my own. The Universe is there, I know. I have some supportive people around me and the time to make this happen is right now.

I know that there are some things I need to do so that, eventually, my parents will understand me. But I don't know what to do in this moment because I'm just too tense right now. I wish they would understand and be supportive. But I think they are as scared as I am, and it's not helping. So I am spending a lot of time in Nantes airport in order to get on a plane and fly back to London. Once in London, I will focus on what I need to focus on right now. No fooling around. It is time to step up.

I'm ready to fly back to London even though I am now cross with both my parents. My mom and I exchanged some angry words that I think she may regret saying. But as I prepare to fly back to London, I feel like the umbilical cord has finally been cut. At least I want to cut it now. This is too much!

THE PLANE IS NOT TAKING OFF

I'm still in Nantes. The flight from Air France tried unsuccessfully to take off. We were on the taxi line speeding up and the plane stopped and they said, *"Sorry, but we're not going to take off right now. We have a technical problem."* So I'm back at the Nantes airport. While we were on the runway, I thought to myself, *"Life is too short. What am I doing arguing with my parents?"* So I called both of them, apologized, and now I'm sitting in the plane at the airport, waiting for further instructions.

Well, the flight was just cancelled. I called my mom and asked her if she could come and pick me up. I'm going to stay overnight and get my flight tomorrow morning at 7:45 am. When I called, my mom was ready to go to work. She runs a restaurant. So she said, *"I can't come right now. There's some traffic."* So I said, *"I'm going to call dad."* So there I was, also calling my dad back. I said, *"Well, you know what? No coincidences in life. The flight is not taking off. Where are you?"* And he was not back in La Baule, he was right around the corner! So he's actually going to come and pick me up and then either drop me directly at home or drop me at my mom's restaurant so we can go out for dinner. I don't know which it will be, but I do know that we will definitely talk.

I'm going to have a conversation with my mom and then my dad and make peace with them. I'm definitely a believer that we should be complete with our parents. I wasn't very happy with the angry situation of earlier. I know this is a tipping point; an important time in my life. It is time for me to grow up and have some heart to heart conversations with my parents and make peace, once and for all.

HEALING CONVERSATIONS

My dad picked me up at the airport with his dog Bizou. We just had dinner at a pizzeria, and we had a long conversation. It was a very nice talk. I just love talking with him. We think so alike. We talked about my book, some ideas, and our philosophies about life. We also talked about horses and how actually an animal, be it a horse or another pet, is like the mirror of its owner. And that is clear with my dad's dog, Bizou. His dog has such a rough haircut that he looks just like my dad. It's so funny. My dad is like a hippie. He is so opposite of my mom, who is sophisticated.

It's interesting how Life had chosen a different outcome for me about leaving Nantes. I can see now that before that could happen, I had to heal the relationship with my parents. I had to talk it through and reconnect with them. Because, let me tell you, when I was ready to fly to London earlier, I was pissed off at both of them, and I know they were both pissed off at me. It wasn't looking good. So you see how it goes? Now I'm happy again and feeling more alive after reconnecting with both of them. Yet I still feel like I've cut the cord; that life cord, that umbilical cord.

A NEW BEGINNING

So I'm now back at my mom's place. Yes, it's funny, co-creator, how destiny, how Life has chosen differently. Life decided that I should be here tonight, and here I am. Tomorrow is my big book signing, the official launch of my book.

Tomorrow will be a take off and departure day for me on many levels. At the moment, I really do feel like I am shifting in and out of all this. As I said earlier, I'm a big believer that we should be complete with our parents. I think that we must resolve things with our parents and within ourselves before we can reach for success. That's my own belief.

I AM AN ADULT

Now it's time to go fully for it. I am an adult, and it's time to act like an adult. It is time for communication, for moving forward, and for taking responsibility. It is time for me to engage, so I can achieve the desired results, and I can make that happen while using the power and the magic of consciously applying the Law of Attraction. It is important to be grounded in reality, but still be open to powerful visualizations and dreams in order to realize our full potential as human beings.

A NEW CHAPTER

So I'm going to take on this new chapter with maturity, a sense of grounding, a clear focus on success, and with humility, joy, and gratitude.

Life goes by, and, even if you are not a particularly spiritual person, I think it is important to realize that we are living at a unique time, a unique moment right now on planet Earth. There are so many things we can make happen and so much joy that can be created. So let's stay in the moment, let's release our fears and focus on what's possible. I'm going to constantly remind myself of that and be grateful for what I have right now and the success that is coming.

As Chantal was telling me in one of her emails, *"Lilou, one day you'll be telling the Universe to slow down so that you can appreciate every single moment."* I just love her cheering me on. I am so grateful to have her in my life. She is really an angel on this earth. It is remarkable to have people like that in your life.

THE POWER OF VISUALIZATION

I am visualizing my book launch. I can see the flow, the energy and all the people showing up. I can sense all the connections coming together. I can feel my speech going smoothly as all the words I need to find come easily to me. I will never forget what my friend, Anthony Robbins, taught me when I attended his seminar. I experienced the power of visualization and of conditioning walking on hot coals without burning myself.

He really taught me an amazing lesson about the power of visualization and conditioning before I do something important. So that is why I am doing visualizations tonight for the book launch that will take place tomorrow and for everything that is to come. It creates juice and excitement in the present moment, and then my mind expands. I feel myself becoming more creative. It is the Law of Attraction in action. It is consciously applying those principals, deliberately applying them, and then allowing the magic to unfold. And let me tell you, co-creator, Life is magic. Let me share that magic with you. Let me share with you the enfoldment of magic, of serendipity, of synchronicity, and of bliss.

A MAGICAL LIFE

When an individual allows his or herself to live it, Life is very, very magical. I am not one of those people who can see into the future, but I can see my future, because my future already exists in this present moment. I'm thinking and creating my future right now and I see it as bright, abundant, prosperous, and fully alive. There is a lot of sharing, a lot of joy and tears of happiness. I'm co-creating that right now. I'm co-creating that with Source, and I'm co-creating it with you and it is magical. It does create magic.

Good night, co-creator. *Bonne nuit* as we say in French. I'll see you bright and early tomorrow morning, ready to take off for my flight to London City Airport. Yee haw! My American side comes up here and there. Fun, fun, fun!

FROM DECLARING TO LIVING

I am just off of Gloucester Road walking toward Hyde Park. I have been listening to the declaration I wrote and recorded a few years ago as part of my meditation CD. It is a bonus; a complete declaration. I want to share it with you right now, so I am going to include a transcript of what I recorded at the end of this paragraph. I also think I'll post a video of the declaration. That way, it will not only be my declaration, but it can be yours as well. I wrote it a long time ago, but it feels even more real and more present to me at this moment because I am more open to its beauty. It expresses how I live my life. What's happening right now is just part of that; a prequel from this perspective, and I want to share that with you:

DECLARATION

The purpose of this document is to lay the context and commitment for being in the World. My intention is to have a life full of miracles, abundance, joy, and love. It is a life which promises to bring love and joy to Life. This document is my declaration. It is my source, my , and the context in which I live my life. The context of my life is that Life is abundant, full of miracles, peaceful, and perfect the way it is. I am living in the context that anything is possible out of declaring it, inventing it, living into it. I design my life. I am at the source of its outcome. It is a beautiful and powerful journey. I live a life in a context that human beings are amazing, kind, generous and perfect the way they are... and ready to make a difference. I am present every day to the beauty and variety of people on this planet. Diversity is magnificent, and each of us express God's gift to the World. We are a team and serve as resources to each other to fulfill our dreams. The Universe answers our need right away. Out of saying it, thinking it, visualizing it, we magnetize what we desire. Possibilities are infinite. I create this space for miracles to happen; people, greatness, love, and joy to give and express; heavenly good moments and peace on Earth to take place. I have now given myself permission to be myself and contribute to Mankind. My approval comes from within. I raise the bar of my participation in Life every day. I own my life, put structures of existence in all areas, and I am hungry for life. I am my dream, accomplishment, and promises. I cannot wait to wake up in the morning, play full out, and invite others to play full out. The result of this abundant energy that I bring to Life is self expression, peace, joy, and love. People are moved, touched, and inspired about Life. I declare myself to be a magnificent leader in an ongoing state of growth, gratefulness, empowerment, freedom, and self expression. As a top performer, I think and then act. I increase my knowledge in every single moment and learn from every single situation. Knowledge is power ,and I am thirsty for knowledge. I increase every day my knowledge, my connections, and expertise. I remember that I create my life and the future moment by moment and believing in others and myself. I declare to alter Life itself on my way and spread the seeds of joy and dreams as possible all over the World. All my dreams and declarations are accomplished, fulfilled, and complete. This is true power. My way of being magnetizes money, success, love, power, and generosity naturally and abundantly. I live my purpose. I do something every day that gets me closer to my dreams and the alteration of Life itself. My relationships are empowering. I am kind to others and myself. I love and believe in others and love and believe in myself. I go beyond my resistance, my shyness, or inhibition and head into the marketplace. I focus my mind on my great potential and on my courage, not my fear. I tap into this immense well of potential every day. I risk it all. It feels great because I know I cannot fail. Life will turn out as I believe it will. I am grateful for being blessed. I am grateful for each and every moment of my life and the miracle of Life itself. I deserve what Life offers to me and big opportunities are falling in my lap. My dreams and declaration are being fulfilled.

CHAPTER 3: OPENING OF THE HEART

SMILING AT TOTAL STRANGERS

I just had a short run in Hyde Park. During the run, I was smiling at people along the way. I did that as an exercise to feel the connection. I have to say that while I was smiling, I didn't have the usual independent negative thoughts racing through my head, such as comparing myself to other runners. Instead, when I would cross paths with someone, I would simply smile. So I had all these goose bumps going through my body. It was absolutely amazing. It was a delightful experience. I was fully charging myself and the run was very nice.

HEART-TO-HEART CONVERSATION

I had a bit less than a 30-minute run and then met with Anne-Sophie, and we had a wonderful heart-to-heart conversation. I am learning to open up and see what's going on, and she has this beautiful, loving energy. In fact her energy is similar to Sonia Choquette's, so it's very easy to be with her to laugh, have a good time, and to share. She's very supportive and confident about how the book will turn out. She has amazing intuition, and she just knows that the outcome will be magnificent. She told me, *"You'll see in two weeks, you'll be laughing at this."*

I am really grateful to have her in my life. She described some experiences that she has had, and it was just delightful to be able to talk so openly, share, and be connected. I've been such a lone ranger for so long. I cannot even explain to you how it has felt to always be pretending to be successful and pretending to have it all together. It has been way too stressful and created so much pressure inside of me. It has blocked me from really knowing and learning about other people. It has prevented me from truly connecting and loving. As I was talking with Anne-Sophie, I could feel how we were helping each other, and it's a new step in my life right now.

I believe I will attract more and more people like Anne-Sophie as I allow myself to open up and be more authentic. It's a really beautiful journey, and I feel like I'm experiencing life at a whole other level. I can't believe it took me so long to arrive at this point. I'm very grateful for this moment and for having taken on this journey, because I feel it is going to open up my whole life.

RE-CREATING WITH IMAGINATION

I am so grateful for my friend Anne-Sophie. I have so much to share. This afternoon we were in a neighborhood private park near home, visualizing all the abundance around us and imagining that we were on this blanket. We were laying down on gold, feeling the vibration and the energy all around us. This big tree in the middle was transforming and had leaves of gold. We were just totally re-inventing the whole world around us. There is just so much beautiful flow in realizing the beauty of life. Everything is present right now. Nothing is missing. Life is unfolding amazingly. If you feel that there is a gap, you just have to look again to see that there is none.

BACK IN THE FLOW OF LIFE

I just posted the picture that I took with Anne-Sophie while in the park from her cell phone on my Facebook page. It is really wonderful. And my status is, *"Back in the flow of life."* Then I wrote some text with the photo album, and it is called *"In the Flow"*. I said, *"We are always in the process. The flow never stops. It is around us at all times."* And that is really how it feels. Anne-Sophie was reminding me of that and saying, *"Yes, it's always there. It's already here. Regardless of anything else, there is always a flow."* I do think that sometimes we just imagine that we have stopped it by feeling separate from it. So now I've jumped back in the flow, and I'm enjoying it. It is always here, always around us, all the time. It never really stops, only in our minds.

MY HEART IS RE-OPENING

I cannot even explain how much my heart is open right now and continuing to open. It is just an absolutely amazing feeling when you have held back and haven't truly lived that way all your life. I have had such a fun-filled day. Let me tell you, my friend Anne-Sophie is so much fun. We kept laughing all day; being like kids again. There is nothing better. We were imagining and creating our reality and it was just magnificent. She gets it and then I get it through her. I just love it. She knows what love is. She can express it and explained to me that it is like this conduit, this amazing life force. She sees it so clearly. It's not really about giving and receiving. It is about being at one with others. I so love how she has shared those things with me. I'm so in awe of this amazing new dimension I'm discovering. I know that none of this would have been possible if I hadn't first gone through my money crisis. So I'm very grateful for that. I know a lot more is opening up, and I just wanted to share it with you. I'm on my way back home. It is midnight and bedtime. I send you much, much love. I wish you a wonderful and beautiful night, co-creator.

July 5th

MEET MY GOD FAIRY

Hello, co-creator, it is Sunday and I'm too excited about life to stay in bed, so I'm reading my emails. I'm also thinking about and feeling the abundance everywhere. I really feel the flow and I feel so abundant, so thankful, and so appreciative. In fact, I kind of feel speechlessness. How do you say it? But I am really present to that. I am very thankful for this experience. I posted a fun video yesterday that I filmed with Anne-Sophie. It is called *"Meet My God Fairy"* http://tinyurl.com/godfairy. My only wish is to have an open heart. I could not find any other wish that would fulfill me more than this one! So, from now on, I want to experience life with an open heart. I'm laughing, connecting, and even laughing at myself and my friends.

It is so much fun to feel this way. I had such a delightful day yesterday. Anne-Sophie totally brought me back into the flow of life, and I am so thankful for that. I'm so thankful for this new connection to everyone. It is pure magic. I feel back in alignment with the flow and I'm receiving so many messages of support.

EVERYTHING IS GOLDEN!

I am in the flow. I see abundance everywhere. Everything is golden. I feel the love that is all around me. The sense of connection is amazing. All of it is amazing. Life is just flowing and the flow feels so real that it is nearly palpable. It is truly powerful. I am so thankful to Baptist, Anne-Sophie, Allan Hunter, and Mascha as well as the 100-Day Reality Challenge Community around the world for supporting, loving, and helping me to get back in the flow. I am so deeply grateful for feeling the love and having an open heart again. *You guys have such big hearts, and I feel so blessed to know you. All that you have done and all that you have shared has helped me so much. You have given me my heart back. Now Lilou is back tenfold; infinite-fold. It feels both magical and real at the same time. I just love it.*

RE-EXPERIENCING LIFE

I can see that actually before this time, there was none of that. I had the sense of something being out there, but nothing like what I'm seeing right now. I cannot wait to meet everybody in my life again and re-experience them at a whole other level. It is through your believing in me and loving me that I am who I am right now. It feels great. I now understand that this was something I needed to live through.

You know, I think life is amazing. I could almost end this book right here because I feel I have arrived at the top of the mountain that I mentioned in the closing pages of my first book. I can feel the flow. I can see it everywhere. It is all around. It is about transforming goals and shining out. I am just swimming in the abundance of Life right now. It is an absolutely amazing feeling. My heart was closed, co-creator, for many, many years, so I am deeply grateful for this ride, for this beautiful journey. Right now, my heart is open...and it's perfect.

CHAPTER 4: EXPERIENCING LIFE IN A NEW WAY

GREEN: MONEY AND HEART CHAKRAS

I received an email from a Scottish reader of I Lost My Job and I Liked It regarding the second book. She said, "The color green seems appropriate since they say it is the color of money. Even though, I must admit, I have only seen green money in stories of Donald Duck. I would love to see a yellow one as well later. I'm very much into yellow right now." She's so lovely. I must admit that I love yellow too and yet the idea of a green book cover for this one, as it deals with money and open heart, feels right. The heart chakra is green and money is often associated with green, so I am thinking of sticking to the green color. My first book had a red cover, which also corresponds to the red root chakras, and now I am going into the heart as a consequence of my money quest. I am creating an entire series of books called the "Juicy Living Series". This is the second one of the series and I am sure I will find another book that will associate itself even better with the color yellow.

FROM FINANCIAL HARDSHIP TO HEAVEN ON EARTH

My best friend Daniel just emailed me. I haven't heard from him in a while. He doesn't know what I'm going through right now and I didn't want to tell him. In fact, I was still not going to tell him because Daniel is a very, very generous person. But, because

I had just had such a powerful breakthrough, I decided I simply had to tell him what was really going on. So I wrote him, *"Oh my God, I need to speak to you. I love you, love you, love you, love you. I have been through the hardest financial time of my life and what just happened is a miracle. The result of all this is an open heart. My heart is opening up again and is open now, Daniel. This is so, so amazing what has happened."*

"I have still not physically manifested money, but I see it everywhere. I am swimming in it right now. I'm not sure if you saw my last three videos, but I am coming from very, very far and now, wow, I'm swimming in it. I can feel it. It is nearly palpable and it is magic. I want to thank you for having started me on this path so long ago. You were the first one that opened my heart, and now I feel the entire conduit is open. It is so amazing; so real. This is what is real. I am in heaven on earth."

And then I said, "I love you, so so very much. I'm sending tons and tons of infinite love your way, a huge conduit of it. Open your arms and your heart. Do you feel it? Yes, it is pouring out of me for you. I love you unconditionally. Lilou."

AN OPEN HEART 100-DAY REALITY CHALLENGE

Hello co-creator, I'm meeting my French friend Anne-Sophie now, and I have to say it has been an unbelievable morning. I'm starting to see the entire world from a different perspective, and it's absolutely amazing. That is what happens when you are living from the heart. There is no lack. There is no mess. Abundance is here, there, and everywhere. I feel trusting and loving. And it is an absolute delight to be in this space. So I started to send an email to Laura and Sandy saying that we should think about doing the 100-Day Reality Challenge on the 20th of August. I'm personally doing it, having an open heart, but how about inviting many other people to live from that perspective? How cool would that be?

July 6th

GENEROSITY IS OMNIPRESENT

I had some friends come over, including Anne-Sophie. I met her for lunch and we enjoyed eating leftovers, which I was very happy to be able to share. We really had nothing more than some pasta to which I added olive oil and I said, "*I apologize for the simplicity of the meal.*" But I was very happy to be able to share that with someone, to feed someone, while experiencing so many new, beautiful feelings.

We were invited both days to different barbeques where there was food, wine, and people also pouring generosity and love. So it was an absolutely magnificent weekend. I believe I still have £2.25 ($3.64) in my account, and the Universe has provided for me. I'm really working on trust now. I am trusting that things are happening and coming together just as they should. Everything I need is already here, and it is simply a matter of time until it manifests. I received an email from my friend Daniel and, as usual, he said, *"Well, I've in fact been thinking of giving you a financial gift for a while."* When I read that, part of me was having issues with my trust, and I wanted to say, *"No, this is not going to happen."* But on the other hand, I was very touched by his generosity, and I'm definitely not going to be blocking that. So, if people, friends, and family want to help, I will accept. But I won't be asking. If it is coming from the heart and someone wants to help, I will gratefully accept their help.

SHARING ON VIDEO

I'm having breakfast and I'm considering doing a video on where I am at in this moment. I want to share the love, the discoveries, and everything that has happened. I want to follow the next inspired action from my heart, and then the next and the next.

FALLING IN LOVE WITH EVERYONE

I'm just really falling in love with everyone. It is really, really cool and very refreshing. It is not that my heart was not open before, but this is a whole other experience, let me tell you. Just learning to trust and following that flow is a blessing. I'm looking forward to sharing this right now. I'm doing my best ever video. It will truly be a piece that is coming from my heart and touching the hearts of many, many, many people. It will be insightful, educational, inspiring, juicy, fun. I am committed to stepping up my message to a whole other level now that I have access to my heart and can tap into its wisdom.

ACCEPTING HELP FROM OTHERS

I was actually delighted this morning to learn that more money has come into two of my bank accounts. I now have over $600 that came in from the sale of some eBooks and other smaller ventures. I am going to take that money and put it in my British account. I just sent my flat mate, Henrik, a text message asking if it would be acceptable that I give him a week's worth of the funds I have so far and *"hopefully you'll accept that,"* I went on to say, *"otherwise, if you want, we can find a way."* I feel now, having had the lessons, that I'm coming from a whole different space, so I will accept help from others. I will accept that gratefully. I don't need to prove myself anymore. I have my heart on fire.

So I texted Henrik, and we'll see what he says. I also let him know that he really touched my heart, and I think of his kindness every day. I'm looking for a way to give him that back because it's now been six days, a week so far, and I haven't had any more than what I have now. But if it is a week's worth, then it means I have some extra money to eat healthy foods, and I'm sure more abundance is pouring in. I have no question about that. I am getting very aligned and continuing to remember to trust the process and the Universe. I uploaded this wonderful video called "Living from an Open Heart" and invited people to join the 100-Day Reality Challenge. So yeah, everything is wonderful.

July 7th

UPS AND DOWNS

6:11 pm on July the 7th. What a day. Let me tell you I had so many ups and downs, I didn't even know where I was standing. I woke up with a closed heart, meditated on the heart, went back up, received an email, went back down, called my mom, went back up. Just received great news, went back up, received negative news, went back down. Until the moment came when I totally broke down in tears. But instead of doing my usual crying on my own, I went to see Giada, my flat mate who was here, and we talked for an hour.

BEING VULNERABLE

I was very grateful to be able to speak with Giada as we did. I was grateful to have a friend there for me with whom I could be vulnerable. So that's definitely the shift that's been happening. I am now reaching out and letting people in, even though I was in a place of scarcity, fear, and just feeling terrified for some reason. It also frustrated me to be so far from the heart at that moment. Yes, I have the fears regarding money, but more than that, it was really, *"Oh no, I'm not living in the heart right now."* And I want to feel that high again because it is such a beautiful, natural high. So I was quite down, and then I went back up when I was with Giada. We also spoke about what I could be doing, and she could definitely see me organizing or helping with an event.

DOING LESS, BEING MORE

Baptist gave me a call. He was so in the flow and open hearted. We spoke for about an hour through Skype. By the end of our conversation, I was just so relaxed and back in the heart again. He definitely knows how to put me back in the flow. We talked about the 100-Day Reality Challenge for an open heart, and he found that a great idea.

Baptist was explaining to me, "Lilou, when you are not in the heart, when you are not grounded, centered, and positive, don't even bother doing anything else." He said, "I meditate in the heart. I walk for an hour in the morning." I asked him, "So, when do you do stuff?" and he said, "I do less, but synchronicity happens and the magic flows."

SURROUNDING MYSELF WITH LOVING PEOPLE

I definitely get what Baptist was saying. He explained that he has to bring myself back to that state, and it requires practice. I'm really, really excited about that. He asked to interview me from his studio tomorrow regarding the shift that has happened. Because the shift that happened for me, coming from a closed heart to an open heart, is really what he wants to achieve through the film he is putting together about the powerful wisdom of the heart.

Oh! I feel released. What a change! I think it's so important to surround ourselves with people that are living from the heart. Because, when you are committed to living from the heart, from that point forward you end up attracting people who are in that flow. All right, co-creator, big kiss. Love you. Speak to you soon.

July 8th

A SHIFT HAS HAPPENED

I really do feel that a shift has happened. Things have been clicking a lot easier and faster since the breakthrough that I had, and it has absolutely changed my entire life. Actually, it has changed every single aspect of my life in a different way. Even public speaking is not as scary to me anymore. People's judgments are not there anymore. You see, the thing that is beautiful about being in the heart is that, when you are in that space, you totally reconnect. Separation from other people no longer exists. We are just one.

I NEVER HAD AN INTIMATE RELATIONSHIP

Now I finally see how much I need to rediscover my entire life. I can tell you right now that I've never truly had an intimate relationship. I am able to see that now. My heart has not been open. I've been scared all the way, always protecting myself. It's such a "wow" moment. I cannot express it in words.

THE FINANCIAL CRISIS WAS MEANT TO BE

"Oh my God. This is actually even bigger than I could have dreamed." I am so thankful for having experienced this no money situation because, without that, I would have never realized what I have come to know and arrived at this place in my life right now. I am so grateful. This is the most beautiful thing ever. This is so priceless. I wish this for everyone. Looking back, I really think that the financial crisis in this world was meant to be experienced by so many of us so we could reconnect with our hearts and be reminded of what is truly, truly important in life. There is amazing human potential. I don't think we have fully tapped into it yet. Hard times are unfortunate, but we learn through them, and I think this is the time for us to reconnect with our souls.

BEING AUTHENTIC

If you are reading this book, it is no coincidence! And I hope that you will share it with others. What I have realized is that by being authentic with other people, by having truthful conversations with the people around you, you will create space inside of you, and once it is created, there is nothing else but for that space to be filled with something else. That something else can be Love. So my recommendation to anyone reading this is that you become open to what is possible and share yourself with others because, by doing so, you will discover yourself in a new way and also discover who your true friends are. That is why the love of my friends and everybody else around me has multiplied. I could have never dreamed of this. So much more is pouring out of me now, and it is going both ways. The experience is absolutely magnificent, and I am so very thankful.

July 9th

NOTTING HILL

This afternoon I am meeting with Menna van Praag, the author of *Men, Money and Chocolate*. We are getting together in Notting Hill. First we will meet at a raw food restaurant, and then after I will be interviewing her. Since her story is so inspiring, I am really looking forward to this meeting and also to discovering Notting

Hill. I saw it in a movie with Hugh Grant but have never been there. How juicy is this going to be?

I just completed a heart meditation where I was fully visualizing giving love to all the people in my life right now. It was different, depending on the people to whom I was sending the love, and it was an absolutely beautiful experience.

CO-CREATING FROM THE HEART

I am really looking forward to interviewing Menna this afternoon. I am excited, but at the same time, feeling a bit scared and challenged by the thought of it. As I am stepping outside of my comfort zone, these mixed feelings make me feel so alive. I have to remind myself to trust and go with the flow, letting everything unfold naturally, rather than imposing my vision on things. However, I believe that it is through visualizing, being in the heart, and knowing what we want that we get a clearer idea of what may be possible. Things are coming into fruition more naturally in my life right now. Part of me still wants to create, but from a different point of view. I now want to co-create in communion with the Universe so I can be fully in the moment and see more clearly what is best for me.

GOING WITH THE FLOW

So now I am in a place of allowing, receiving, and giving, instead of just imposing my own images and feelings on things. Because I have already put my desires out there, I am letting go and trusting much more. I am feeling great about what I'm doing and just going with the flow. I've done my part of the job, and now it is just a matter of being open and remaining open.

BEING IN LOVE WITH LIFE

I'm going to do a video about the experience of having an open heart and being in love with life. It is just a wonderful, amazing feeling, and I want to share it with many more people. I'm thinking maybe I might even do some shorter videos that are like Twitter messages, but in video form. I think that's what is missing; a little glimpse of things. I can imagine many videos of about one minute 40 seconds in length, equal to 100 characters of text. There's a lot to be said for that. I just have ideas about how I can co-create a project on the open heart. I'm doing the open heart 100-Day Reality Challenge and I am feeling very creative right now, so I'm just getting ready.

My interview with Menna is prepared. I am now physically getting in gear and will then do the videos. It is time to have some lunch. I am sending you much love.

BEING GUIDED BY THE HEART

It was so lovely meeting Menna van Praag in Notting Hill. She is wonderful. I absolutely love her and how she lives with an open heart. That is the message of her book. That is also the message we got across in the videos and I look forward to sharing them. It was a lot of fun, and I feel blessed to have met her. We spoke about how she attracted her publisher and how she also always knew in her heart that they would be her publisher. However, hearing her story, I felt grateful for the way my journey has been unfolding. I feel truly blessed. I'm not sure things would be any better with a publisher.

I am just taking it one moment at a time, living from the heart, and letting that guide me. Having a publisher is something good, I think, but not the solution to my money problem or to any other problem. I think there is something juicier in store!

PLAYING SMALL DOES NOT SERVE THE WORLD

At this point, I want to share a beautiful message with you from Marianne Williamson. You have probably read or heard it before. This is a truly special one, isn't it?

"Our deepest fear is not that we are inadequate. Our deepest fear is that we are powerful beyond measure. It is our light, not our darkness, that most frightens us. We ask ourselves, Who am I to be brilliant, gorgeous, talented, and fabulous? Actually, who are you not to be? You are a child of God. Your playing small does not serve the world. There is nothing enlightened about shrinking so that other people won't feel insecure around you. It's not just in some of us, it's in everyone. And as we let our own light shine, we unconsciously give other people permission to do the same."

Read those words one more time and let their meaning sink deep down inside of you.

"…Who am I to be brilliant, gorgeous, talented, and fabulous? Actually, who are you not to be? You are a child of God. Your playing small does not serve the world."

Yes, I definitely agree with that. I am going to put that message on my computer right now!

THE MAGIC OF LIVING FROM THE HEART

The magic of living from the heart is really fabulous and fascinating. It simply blows my mind. Things flow, ideas come, and Life is fully aligned. You no longer need to worry what your purpose and passion is in life. Life just flows. It's simply up to you to stay in that flow and bring it all together.

I started out wanting to attract money and that led me to opening up my heart, and I now truly believe that the money is going to show up very soon.

I'm starting to get back in the flow and this is making it possible for me to attract successful ideas and amazing things into my life.

A WARM BUBBLY BATH

Ah, co-creator. I'm relaxing in a warm, bubbly bath with two red candles on either side and it's absolutely delicious. The temperature of the bath is perfect. I was inspired by a message I received from Mimi, one of the co-creators on Facebook (Facebook.com/LilouMacewebTV). She sent me a message suggesting that I check out a video that Julia, another co-creator (from France) put together for her. Watching Julia's video inspired me to actually meditate in the bath. So right now, I'm getting ready to do a heart meditation from my bath. Ah, it is so lovely.

GOING UP, UP, UP ON AMAZON

Sonia Choquette has just sent a newsletter to her mailing list featuring *I Lost My Job and I Liked It* as the selected book of the month. In just two hours, the book went up to an 11th ranking on Amazon.com, which reflects a sales ranking of 11,000. So that means that out of all the books that are sold on Amazon right now, my book is being recognized as selling in the 11th ranking, and it is climbing. I keep updating my Facebook page information about it, and I am receiving many positive messages.

So, I'm keeping my fingers crossed, but I do feel that the momentum is building and I'm going to do everything I can to continue that strong flow of energy. Right now, I'm going to do a special meditation that sends a lot of light and love to the book. Alright, my co-creator, I'm enjoying this already.

I'm quite excited to discover that on Amazon in France, my book is listed as number 863 for an English language book. It's actually listed as number seven in the Job Hunting and Career category, and number thirty-nine in the Health, Mind, and Body category. How cool is that, co-creator? It is in seventh place of most books sold! That is really exciting! I have to take a screenshot picture of that page. The book is climbing up and up in sales!

July 11th

I LOVE THE NUMBER 11

I'm awake in the middle of the night and realized that it is the 11th of July, co-creator. I love the number 11. And I'm not so surprised now that I am so in the flow with an open heart and am seeing magic take place. I began to see this shift happen from the moment I opened my heart. It is just one thing leading to another, and it is now like a chain letter of people helping.

IT HAS ONLY BEEN A WEEK!

From the moment I opened my heart, my life has been filled with synchronicities and amazing events, one after the next. My life was already pretty extraordinary and a lot of fun. I had lots of joy and no complaints. But now this; it is truly remarkable, co-creator.

Also, I spent a wonderful time with my friend, Anne-Sophie, this afternoon. We talked about how great life is and all sorts of mystical things.

I couldn't believe that it has only been a week since all this happened. It feels like months have passed!

MY SKIN CONDITION

Since I have been in England, I have had a problem with a skin condition on my face. I think it has been stress-related. This is new to me. I did not have acne growing up and now as an adult, my skin is starting to act strange and flare up. It is more like a skin inflammation problem.

A PURPLE HEART

I talked with Anne-Sophie and updated her about my latest amusing conversations and adventures. She then said, *"Did you check in your room? There's a present for you."* When I checked, Anne-Sophie had left this little red box with a beautiful purple ribbon on it for me. It was absolutely magnificent because I had told her that purple is my spiritual color. Then, when I opened the little box, inside was a beautiful necklace. It was a light purple color in the shape of a heart. Also inside the red box was a note that read: "*Le monde en or,* which, translated into English, means: *"The world is gold."* How precious. What a beautiful gift. It totally touched my heart. I will remember the opening of the heart with her forever. I am blessed.

July 12th

RUNNING 15K

I'm walking toward the tube station. I'm going to do a 15K run today. I had a good breakfast and now we'll see what happens because 15K seems quite a bit. I can manage an hour and 15 minutes or an hour and 30 minutes, but this is the maximum run I can do. I don't want to push it too hard. Later this afternoon, I'm also playing tennis with Anne-Sophie. So it's quite a sportive day. I've been meditating. It always feels good re-opening the heart and living from the heart all day long, one minute at a time.

NOT BEING SEPARATED FROM ABUNDANCE

We need to understand that money and abundance and everything that life has to offer is in non-separation; is in oneness. If I'm not feeling separated from the abundance that is there, that is because there is no separation. It comes from the understanding that we are all part of Source Energy. We are love, and when we are in the flow of love, things happen. It is all about trusting, believing, and allowing.

FEELING THE ABUNDANCE

I can now very easily see and feel all the abundance. It is like all the streets are transforming into gold and there is this magic. I also now know that it's beautiful to see the flow and how everything that we want and desire is there in an unmanifested state. It's just a matter of aligning with that vibration and allowing it to come into the manifested state. I just arrived home. I'm going to take a bath and meditate a bit more because my legs are feeling heavy after all the exercise I had today. The sun is shining. It's a beautiful day, and I give thanks for all the abundance that is coming into my life.

July 13th

PRACTICING WHAT I HAVE LEARNED

I woke up very relaxed this morning, but then, after looking at my financial situation, I got stressed again. My US bank account is negative. I don't have much in the UK account either, but there is enough for me to still go shopping for some food right now. That is good. I'm very thankful for that.
I did a heart meditation and practiced all that I have been learning lately.

THY WILL BE DONE

There is a saying in the Bible, *"Thy will be done."* In French, it is *"Ta volonté soit faite"*. Repeating those words helps us to wake up and be thankful for our soul. So there is a lot of surrendering and trusting at the same time. When we say those words, we have to really mean them. This incantation causes our whole being to vibrate at an intensity that provokes our soul to once again awaken. I tried it this morning and it wasn't that easy.

FIRST, GET BACK IN THE FLOW

I think I'm going to spend a bit of time in the park, in nature. As much as I feel like doing other things, I know that first, I need to get back into the flow so I can access the feeling of oneness. The park is a good place to do that, because in the city, there are just too many distractions.

PANIC ATTACK

This is crazy. I'm totally freaking out. The co-creating area of the domain name is down. The Lilou Mace domain is down. There must be some kind of problem with my bank card. I'm totally in a panic zone. I'm just going to take some deep breaths in the park and then see what next step I am led to take.

I SURRENDER

I'm really, really stressed. I took off my flip flops and just started circling this little park. It is actually more like a big garden when you are in the middle of it, and it's located in a very nice neighborhood. I think it is so beautiful and heavenly here. So I just started walking and walking and walking and walking; letting go of my stress. And then I started singing, *"I surrender, I surrender all."*

GARDENING

As I was walking in the park, I saw the gardener. He is an older gentleman, probably retired. He does everything so delicately in the park all the time. So I felt inspired to ask him if I could help him. I still had some things on my mind, but I thought it would be really great if I could spend some time working in the park and he said, *"Yeah, sure. Why don't you pick up the leaves?"* So here I am now, with one of those huge rakes, grabbing all the old leaves. He asked me to go around on the path because there's a beautiful path around the park, and so I'm doing that right now. I'm gathering up the leaves, and it feels really good. As I was doing that, I was also reconnecting with my soul. I felt like the Karate Kid, but instead of having an instructive time, it felt like Life was telling me, *"Okay, now it's time to pick up the leaves."* (Laughter)

RECONNECTING WITH MY SOUL

All right, this feels great. I'm reconnecting with my soul as I am picking up those leaves. I felt very grateful for that and thanked the Universe. And now I'm continuing to do some more. I feel better. For me, it's more effective than just walking as it is keeping my mind busy. I can see why some people garden every day. I'm very thankful to have access to this little garden and the chance to reconnect with nature.

STRONG FEARS

I had so much fear that came crawling right back in, that I nearly couldn't breathe. I don't think I have ever felt a strong fear like this in my whole life. So I called my friend Amarun. She said, *"Be with it. Be with that fear. Do something else. Just go out there."* So I did. I went to Hyde Park and just walked and walked. At one point I even laid down and actually slept, but the fear was still there. So I just talked to it, I embraced it, I thanked it, and I cried. Then, all of a sudden, I had the thought, *"Why am I being so hard on myself? Why am I trying to punish myself with this?"*

FINDING SOLUTIONS FROM A LOVING PLACE

And then I saw how much I always come up with solutions regarding money when I'm in a place of fear or scarcity instead of just a loving place. So I want to find a solution now from a place of love. I saw a beautiful tree in Hyde Park, and when I looked down, there was £1 ($1.62) on the ground. Then I turned around and found another tree that I could climb, so I climbed it. I engraved in the tree "Lilou" with a big heart around it. I felt so happy up there. It was magic.

I'm still looking for a solution, and how to be responsible for where I'm at, but I want it to come from a place of love. So I'm being gentle with myself.

POEMS ON FEAR

After sharing what I was going through with Baptist, he sent me this poem via email entitled, *I Love and Embrace My Fear*.

I embrace my fear.
I will face my fear.
I allow my fear to be.
I am grateful for my fear.
I will allow my fear to pass over and through me,
I will let my fear be.
I love my fear.
Thank you so much.
And when it has gone past,
I will turn the inner eye
to see its path
Where the fear has gone,
there will be nothing.
Only I will remain.

I thought that was very beautiful, and so I was inspired to write my own little poem.

I was afraid,
my fear was here.
I looked within,

I saw more fear.

I thanked my fear and it disappeared.

I felt love that had been here.

I found myself within my fear.

A FEAR VIDEO

Alright co-creator, I just recorded a video blog describing my fear. Here is the link to that video: http://tinyurl.com/dealingwithfear. I want to share myself authentically. My videos are real!

The weather is absolutely beautiful. I want to thank you for hanging in there with me, co-creator. I promise you that something stunning and juicy will come out of all this! I send you much love.

PAINTING RAINBOWS

I'm on my way back home, meeting Anne-Sophie, and we're going to do a painting of a beautiful rainbow and some other things that I can use for the backdrop when I record my videos. How fun is that? It is a beautiful, lovely evening. I haven't found the solution I need as yet, but we'll see what unfolds as time goes by, co-creator. I've got some things to deal with, and I know that I will make something happen.

July 14th

NURTURING THE INNER CHILD

It is 6:00 am, and I have been awake because the fear is here with me. Yesterday evening I had a lovely time with Anne-Sophie when we did some painting. We painted a beautiful rainbow, and we shared some very special moments. But my fears keep crawling right back in, so I'm not sure what to do, co-creator. I need to find a solution. I would love to be able to stay here in London, but I don't know what is going to happen.

Finding vibrational alignment is much needed right now, but when there is so much fear, it is hard to do! I'm just trying to reassure my inner child that we will find a solution. I wonder why on one hand, I feel so powerless, and on the other hand, I feel so high? I'm asking myself a lot of questions. To bring myself into vibrational alignment is there something I am missing that I need to see?

Thy will be done!

FINDING A NEW SOLUTION

Okay, I just posted an ad on A Small World: *"Looking for a London flat for six weeks this summer?"* I really believe it will attract someone exceptional. It will be the perfect time for someone, and this way I can live somewhere else that I can afford.

FEAR: False Evidence Appearing Real

I just received a message from Mary. She lives in Holland and we met at the Mariana's wedding. She just posted a blog on FEAR: "False Evidence Appearing Real." That was something that I spoke of in my first book. I just read her blog because it was a message that I needed to receive right now.

Here is what Mary said, "I thought this was beautiful and a great reminder for when fears come up. The credit goes to Ruth Fishel from the book Peace in Our Hearts, Peace in the World, FEAR: False Evidence Appearing Real."

"Fear is natural and healthy. Fear can save our lives. When the car drifts unexpectedly into our lane, we swerve quickly to avoid an accident. When something threatens us, fear shouts at us to provoke self-protection action.

But so many of our fears are born in our thoughts and not in reality. We project our fears into a future that does not exist. We imagine scenes where the worst happens. We make ourselves physically ill by stressing our body with scenarios that exist only in our mind. How much gentler to ourselves can we be when we learn to say no to our projected thoughts, to stay in the present moment where we can shine a light upon reality. That way our fears have no place to go. Then each moment can become a moment of peace rather than a moment of stress."

July 15th

PUTTING OURSELVES BACK IN THE FLOW

It is 11:00 am on the 15th of July, and I'm truly realizing how much we have to take responsibility for putting ourselves back into the flow. Nobody else is going to do it. It's up to each of us. If we're really fearful and upset, it is about finding release and then getting back into the flow. So that is what I'm practicing. I'm now on my way to meeting Simon. He is someone that my friend Marla wants me to meet. I'm looking forward to the conversation that will take place.

CREATING INTENTIONS

I've got a copy of my book with me and my intention is to allow my spirit and soul to experience this fully and completely with an open heart.

It is good to have an open heart. With positive intention, you allow some important changes to take place, which lead to clearing out negativity. Once you make the most of it, you are going to open up to a lot of things that needed to be opened up.

My intention is to be successful. I want to have a balanced life and have amazing people in my life. I want to be really tight and connected with my family and to always take the time for them. Most importantly, I want to love myself unconditionally every single step of the way. I declare with an open heart that I love and believe in myself. I love and believe in others and I allow all great things to come into my life.

SUSTAINABLE SUCCESS

What I am trying to achieve here is sustainable success. Not just a one-night stand success, but a lifelong success. I know you can relate to this. When we go through hard times, that is when long-term goals really come into focus, and that is what we are talking about here. There is major work to be done, but every little thing that we do along the way adds up; it all counts. It could be one meeting. It could be one conversation with a stranger. It could be one phone call that you make. It could be one book that you read. It could be one e-mail that you send out. It could be one smile that you share. It could be one moment of eye contact. It could be one simple step that you take with an open heart.

If we just let things happen, if we trust and we allow things to unfold, Life can bring us all sorts of magic. I have a feeling that this is about to happen. Maybe it's going to take place on a plane, on the street, in a bar, in a café, or at a networking event. I think it's important to follow our hearts because, once we do that, we begin to pick up on our own strong, beautiful gut feelings that something amazing is out there.

SONIA'S WISDOM

I watched Sonia Choquette's video this morning about why we are here. It is in three parts on YouTube. When you type her name in YouTube, you will see my interviews with her on meditation, fear, negativity, and more. I think she is a wonderful teacher, and I was very inspired by her video. I want you to pay attention to all these small things coming together. When you have achieved one small thing successfully, everything else falls into place and it can happen very quickly. Are you ready?

Right now, for me, one small little thing was smiling at a total stranger, the next was putting on a bit of lip gloss, and the next was another smile. Now, here I am on Fulham Road not far from Nero Café where I am meeting Simon.

MEETING SIMON

I just met with Simon. He is best friends with the famous artist, Sting. Let me tell you, Simon is an unusual, unsettling, and funny character. He greeted me by saying, *"I can see you're not grounded at all. You're all over the place."* At first I was like, "*Uh-oh, what is this?*" Let me tell you, when somebody that you have just met throws that at you, your mind starts running wild. From my reaction, he probably saw that I didn't know where he was coming from, and that is when he told me that he was a student of spirituality.

After he said that, I relaxed a bit as I knew that, to some degree, he would have an open mind. This also led to his asking me questions about how I put my book together. Then he rapidly changed subjects telling me that he wants to sell his place in London and buy one in Oxford. As I had gone to Oxford Brookes University, the atmosphere he was describing brought back memories to me. At that point, we were connecting and relating for the first time in our conversation. He shared with me how sometimes he drives there to resource, re-energize, refresh, fill his spirit, and relax. I'm like, *"Yeah, that sounds wonderful,* and immediately suggested, *"We should do that now."* So, there I was, offering to drive up to Oxford with this 'near' stranger. I was ready to cancel all my appointments for the day and just do it. It felt right in my heart. I could just imagine the wonderful energy Oxford would bring into my life. It felt so appropriate at that moment so I reaffirmed, *"Yeah, let's go. Let's go there."*

PLANNING LUNCH IN OXFORD

Instead Simon and I made plans to go to Oxford on Monday for lunch and then come back. He said he would drive us up there. How cool is that? It was definitely better than traveling by train! I shared my story with him and, at some point, when I told him more about my book, he asked me, *"So, are you in bookstores?"*

That led to my being very open with him about my situation. I told him, "*I am up against the wall right now. I don't have the money to print books.*" I saw him thinking. He is obviously very well off and, for a second, I thought he was going to propose giving me the money!

Then he asked me, "*What did you think when we were going to meet? What did you think of it?*" I told him that I was expecting a conversation that could lead to a shift of some kind. I shared my view of life with him, how I believe that everything happens for a reason, and that our meeting felt like synchronicity. So, on Monday, the 20th, I'm going to go to Oxford with Simon.

PRE-CELEBRATION OF THE SECOND BOOK

I just came back from a party, and I have to say I've never seen so many people in London at one time that I knew. There were people that had attended my events and many friends. It was just unbelievable. I had a lovely time there. Free champagne was pouring. I felt so abundant! So I see this as a pre-celebration for my second book, the same way I had a pre-celebration for my first book. But the difference is that the last time I could afford to buy the champagne myself and this time, I could not. ;) LOL! And let me tell you, there was an abundance of champagne.

Now I'm walking on Regent Street to get back home, co-creator. I'm on one of the most prestigious avenues of London and I'm very thankful for this evening. I met some great people and passed around my business card, which has the image of my book cover on the front and my contact information on the back. I love the synchronicity of things, and I can definitely see the Universe working even harder than I am. I love it! That's the flow of life.

July 16th 2009

GOING BACK TO FRANCE

Going to France might be the best option for me at this point, but I don't know for sure. Earlier I was feeling confused about whether I should rent my room in London and move back to France or if I should stay in London and try to attract money right now. But it feels more and more right for me to go back to France for the summer, so I'm going to check how it feels on a soul level and ask the wise part of me for guidance.

Einstein said it very well: "The intuitive spirit is a sacred gift; the rational mind, its faithful servant. But most people have thrown away the gift and have become enslaved to the servant. The intuitive spirit is who you really are. It is your essence, and it is alive, and it lives in the heart."

GETTING CLEAR ON A SOUL LEVEL

I now feel clear on a soul level what the next best step is for me. It is definitely to go to my parents in France, be with my mom, and connect with my soul. In the past, I've had lots of hard times with my mom, so on an intellectual level, I feel that going back to my mom is going to be a disaster because we clash all the time. That is the reason I felt led to move to the US at the end of my studies. But now, connecting with the heart and seeing the bigger picture about how much the money plug has been totally pulled out, I am making a deeper connection and decision. What's really important for me is to work on healing. So I will follow that guidance, at least for now. This is how I feel and this is what feels right.

HEART VERSUS MIND

I remind myself that the ego is a personal assistant and not the big boss! As scared as I am right now with the situation, I'm remembering that there are always two conversations. There is the conversation with my heart and the conversation with my mind. So I can now see, on a soul level, that this is what was needed, and I'm grateful for the opportunity to grow and to be guided in a different direction. My US bank account is in the negative, so I'm checking my British account and the business account. But most importantly, what I am doing right now is getting back to a place of gratitude, being in the moment, and being in the heart, even with no money.

MAKING THE IMPOSSIBLE BECOME REALITY

I just watched the film, *Man on Wire*. You have got to see it! It's about this Frenchman that crossed between the Twin Towers in New York City on a high wire. It's so inspiring! It was his dream since he was a child and he did it. I'm very, very inspired right now. I found the story fascinating and everything was well documented. It was just so brilliant. My flat mate, Henrik, had the DVD of the film at home and told me about it. He said that I had to watch it, and now I can see why. It shows that, regardless of all the obstacles this guy had, he just went for it and made (what seemed) an impossible dream come true! How amazing and mind blowing. After watching this film, my inspiration has definitely reached a new height.

July 17th

PAINTING

Last night I did this playful, beautiful painting. I felt inspired to do something artistic, so I took the brush and some ink that Anne-Sophie had left behind after one of her visits. The painting turned out great and it is something that will make a wonderful background that I can use in my videos if I want to do so. This morning, I started my day with an open heart meditation. I just sat there for maybe 10 or 20 minutes trusting my heart and opening up.

INNER GUIDANCE

I asked my heart some questions regarding my living situation because, as you know, I'm still debating about what I should do next. I kept on questioning my heart and paid close attention to the feelings that came up; whether they were warm or aching or coming from anxiety. I just remained open to the solutions that asking questions of my heart would inspire.

SHARING MY YOUTUBE EXPERIENCE

I'm really excited to speak about my YouTube experience at a seminar today, co-creator. It makes perfect sense. I'm putting the intention out there that, at this seminar, there will be lots of people wanting to connect and do some things, such as organize events, paid events, with me very soon. I have prepared something that I think is definitely going to take more than the hour and a half that I have been given. There is lots of content, lots of tips, and lots of information.

I visualized myself sending love to all the people that will be attending, a really full room, and lots of excitement. I will be speaking from the heart. This is my first such seminar and it is so exciting! I should be nervous, but I'm not because this is a new experience, a new adventure, and a new way to connect with more people. For that reason, the seminar will be even more powerful, have more energy, and more love.

SPEAKING FROM THE HEART

What a shift! I had the most amazing experience ever doing the seminar with an open heart. I had such a great connection with people while exchanging information and just talking. It was like doing a dance and I was showing my elements. I'm so grateful. What a change from where I was a month ago at my book signing. My level of communication and connection took a quantum leap. So I feel quite drained right now and I'm recharging my battery. I'm going back home. Good night, co-creator!

HE IS THE ONE!

I just had a conference call with Philippe in Germany. He was the first person who replied to the ad that I posted on A Small World website to find a roommate, and he's absolutely perfect. I knew from the beginning that he was the one. Then we did a little video conference so that Henrik could meet him and it went really well. He's going to give us the answer on Monday, but yeah, it's another relief. It is as easy as that when you're in the flow! You just know it by following intuition. There is no need for additional check-ups. It feels right in the heart. I know now I am supposed to move to my mom's home in France.

SIX MONTHS LATER...

CHAPTER 5: THE FLOW

January 19th 2010

It's about 2:00 pm here in France, and I'm really excited about sharing some good news with you! It has been nearly six months since we have spoken. So here is where I am at and what is unfolding.

I have been living at my mom's home in France since October of last year. It feels good to be here and get close to her. We have many things to talk about. France is also definitely a great place to open my heart and to further this work until I have a stable financial situation. I'm just really happy being here and enjoying an abundant quality of life. It has not been easy every day, but this is what felt good and what I had to do for now. It is humbling.

This book is particularly focused on that; abundance, prosperity, and enjoying all the greatness that the Universe offers. It is all right in front of us, but most of the time, we don't even open ourselves to this greatness, to this natural flow. We don't take the time to co-create with the Universe to the best of our abilities.

FINDING BALANCE

I have just received more very exciting news. A Japanese publisher is interested in my book *I Lost My Job and I Liked It*. I self-published it and now Light Works, a Japanese publisher, has just made an offer. I feel really abundant and grateful. So this is why I'm excited. But I know that sometimes when I'm too excited, life brings some less happy news to balance things out. Do you know what I mean?

I think it's very important to stay in a neutral zone or, as some people call it, *"point zero."* You must stay in balance as much as possible and not go into those big highs because sometimes you can then go into the big lows. So I'm working on that balance and trying to ground myself.

NO MORE SELF-SABOTAGE

I really feel the timing is right. I'm opening myself up to the abundance and to the magnificence that life offers. I am reminding myself of this now as, in the past, I always cut myself short, self-sabotaged myself. I'm done with that. It was part of my old karma, part of the past. Now a shift of consciousness is happening in the world, and I'm not relating to money in the same way. I'm not relating to myself in the same way. I've grown tremendously and have opened my heart. So now it's about continuing in this process and sharing that with you. I love you beautiful co-creators. Speak to you very soon!

BOOSTING MY VIBRATION

Here's a little trick I use to boost my vibration and attract more powerfully. This is when we co-create with the Universe. By consciously applying The Law of Attraction and raising my vibration, I get to manifest what I want even faster. When I was a kid, I always used to do that instinctively. Didn't you?

I would love to work with Trédaniel and with the Japanese publisher so I told myself that if I sign this contract, I'll get a professional massage. It may sound conditional, but I see it as a playful game rather than an obligation. This adds extra positive energy to the manifestation, and therefore becomes more real on some levels. It's already exciting to think of signing a book contract with a publisher, but associating the massage to the signing, makes it even more real. The massage is something I can relate to, and I know how good it feels, therefore, it raises my vibration. It works for me. I think we all use those little tricks at times, and they are important to use because it's really about raising our vibration and feeling good about whatever we want to manifest.

OUR INFINITE POWER

I believe we can all manifest a lot of things very easily. This is part of the power and abilities that we were given when we were born. We can tap into that infinite power by opening our hearts, by trusting, and by following our inner guidance and intuition. Once we do that, things unfold naturally and magically. I have had and will continue to have many occasions to put this into practice, and I will share my experiences with you in this diary.

January 20th

ASKING MY SOUL FOR GUIDANCE

I had a great day. It's about 11:26 pm, and I'm in bed. Before closing my eyes, I'm asking one question of my soul. *"Please help me to clarify how I can bring abundance to my life?"* I think bedtime is a great time to ask ourselves these questions as during the night when you are asleep, your soul travels to get the answers that you need and then your mind transcribes them in a thought, a dream, or a new idea that comes to you when you wake up. I am also doing my gratitude list in my head. The things I'm grateful for today.

January 21st

WE FORGOT WHERE WE COME FROM

Allowing, welcoming, opening the heart; this is what I feel is important. We are just amnesic. We have forgotten who we really are, forgotten our potential. We have forgotten our vibrancy and that our essence is love.

When we're not attracting what we want, it is because we are resisting. It's that resistance, those negative thoughts, those doubts, that are not permitting natural abundance and manifestations to flow in. We have so much infinite power. It's ridiculous. It's beautiful. It's magnificent. It's divine. But we have forgotten all this. I think it is time for us to remember and re-open ourselves to this gift.

SURRENDERING

We're co-creators, and so I'm going to allow and make welcome more and more in life. We often hear about surrendering, but I never understood the full feeling of it. I really prefer the terms allowing, accepting, and opening the heart. That resonates for me and feels right.

I'm sharing my thoughts in the process as they come to my mind, and I'll put them in action if it feels right. You too will find the right formula. I'm not saying I have the answer. What I'm saying is that I'm willing to play the game of life. I'm willing to learn and grow and to be this human being, this spirit here on earth, as fully as possible. I'm living my mission with passion, juiciness, and enthusiasm.

THIS IS GOING TO BE A BAD DAY!

I just had a small argument with my mom and right now living with her is not easy. She just asked what I ate yesterday night. She is always checking the food and always needs to know. That really annoys me. I just got into a negative mood swing. When I woke this morning, I was very open and all of a sudden, boom… this incident happens and changes everything. We all have those incidents that can happen first thing in the morning or during the day that make us think, *"Oh, this is a bad day"*.

After checking my email, receiving a disappointing message, and having the argument with my mom, my mind just went into a negative loop. There we go again! When we anticipate having a bad day, then everything that comes in, we interpret negatively.

REALIGNMENT

Thank God for this journal. Thank God for my being in the process of allowing today, for accepting and wanting to welcome more, and opening up to abundance because I'm not going to let negativity run the show.

So how do I realign myself now from the negative vibration? One way is by sharing how I feel with you as I'm doing right now. This really helps. I could have done this via a video blog, but instead I am recording a voice memo. This really helps me. I'm also going to do a "let go" meditation. This will remind me that I am one with everything, including the plant right here in front of me.

By reconnecting to this infinite source, breathing in, and reopening up to the abundance, life starts to flow back again and we shift. Yes, it's a day by day, hour by hour, minute by minute, second by second, thought by thought process. So I'm declaring for myself that I will live an abundantly beautiful day.

UNDERLYING THOUGHTS

Now, when I say these words, if I'm being really honest, I'm thinking, *"Yeah right!"* What is really happening is that I am having other thoughts running parallel to the positive one, and they are saying, *"Yeah right. Well, this hasn't been proven in reality…in your reality. This is not a good start, so what is really going to happen today?"* How do I override that? Again, it's about shifting the experience. So I need to sit down and take the time to open myself up to the abundance and remember where I am coming from. I need to remind myself that I am loved and open my heart again.

MONEY HUNGRY

I do not want to do any job for money reasons alone. I'm done with that, hence my previous book. In the US, I was money hungry and it was one of the most important focuses for me at the time. When I was afraid that I would not be able to pay the bills, I would accept jobs that were not exciting to me with clients I did not really like working for. The thing to remember here is that we always have a choice, even when it does not look like we have one! That is the real reality.

I believe if we see that life is abundant, then abundance shows up in every way. So, the more I'm opening myself up to that, the more I think synchronicities like these are just going to happen naturally. Then the seeds that I have planted will pop up and come out of the earth. You never know which ones, but that makes it fun too!

NO OTHER ALTERNATIVE

It's just a matter of time before I get some proposals and offers, whether it's for the book or for TV or for interviewing other authors. I see no other option because of the enthusiasm, the love, and the time I put in it. I'm not doing this for any reason other than the fact that I really love what I do. Yes, I do have some objectives and goals in mind, but they are not my driving force. My biggest drive, my biggest intention, is to help people and to do what I'm here to do…to do what I love doing, which is interviewing, informing, encouraging, and inspiring. So, yes, as a consequence of my actions and my intentions, opportunities will come to me.

For now, paid or not, I'm just spending my time doing what I love. I love this too much to stop. This is so much an extension of what I'm meant to do here. I got really clear about that while I was writing my first book, hence this second book.

WAITING ON THE NEXT SYNCHRONICITY

I placed a Post-it note on my computer that says, *"Are you waiting on the next synchronicity?"* This reminds me that by actively listening and waiting for the next synchronicity, magic will happen. I received this practice from James Redfield, the author of *The Celestine Prophecy*. He is an internationally bestselling author. His book was number one for all of 1995 and then number two in 1996. I interviewed him after I interviewed Carl Calleman, an expert on the interpretation of the Mayan calendar. James Redfield had found my interview with Carl Calleman, loved it, and then contacted me. If you would have told me a year ago that James Redfield would contact me, I would have told you that you were insane. This is all much bigger than I could have dreamed.

In that interview (which you will find on YouTube and lilouMace. com) he said if you open up, you'll be rewarded. He went on to say that being in integrity with ourselves and people around ourselves is crucial here. It is important to just clean up, clean up, clean up as it comes and forgive ourselves and forgive others.

Anyway, I'm off to the gym after all of this, co-creator, and waiting on the next synchronicity. Love you…love, love, love, love, love, love, love, love. I'm singing love!

BEDTIME GRATITUDE LIST

It's now midnight and bed time, so I am going to close my eyes and be grateful for all the wonderful things that have happened today, including having the possibility to go to the hairdresser.

I had a lot of beautiful highlights put in so I'm very grateful for that. I'm grateful for having spent some time with my mom and having dinner with her on my way back here. I'm grateful for all the wonderful interviews that I'm doing. I'm grateful for having a warm bed to sleep in. I'm grateful for being tired and knowing that I'm going to have a wonderful rest. I'm grateful for surrendering and opening my heart more each day. I'm grateful for the beauty, the magnificent of this planet. I'm grateful for living in this present moment in time to see the evolution of consciousness and people opening their hearts more and more. I'm grateful to be part of the people that are helping that shift. I'm grateful for the knowledge that I have acquired on the internet that enables me to have created the Web TV, being self-sufficient enough to launch it, do videos, and be able to have the contacts and the network that I'm creating here in France so fast. I'm grateful to be guided by the Source every day. I'm grateful for doing what I love. I'm grateful for you. I'm grateful for doing this second book. I'm grateful for my pillow right now. I'm going to go to bed. Good night, co-creator.

January 22nd

I LOVE YOU, LILOU

It's 7:00 am and I'm awake so I'm going to get out of bed. This is a little bit early, but I have had sufficient sleep. I'm so present to the love that I feel. I said to myself, "*I love you, Lilou. I love you.*

I love you so much." And I feel that love growing. It's amazing. I never could have said that before, but the more I give myself the love that I've always been seeking, the more respect I have, and the more love grows inside and outside of me for myself and for other people. It is really magnificent and I think this is part of the process of attracting abundance. Being in abundance is embracing who you are with your weaknesses and your strengths. Love balances it all. So, I'm just really present to that growing love. When I said to myself, *"I love you, Lilou,"* I really meant it and felt unconditional love. It does not come from pride or from feeling that I'm better than anyone else. It is just pure love, deep respecting love, and it is growing.

VIBRATION VERSUS PRODUCTION

It is 7:00 pm. I had a pretty productive day but again; I don't want what I produce to relate to a schedule, but instead to how I vibrate. So on a vibrational level, I would say I was at a six or seven. I could definitely do better on a scale of zero to 10. I was on and off. I wasn't totally in the flow. Right now I am in the flow, but I wasn't that way all day. I even had a little nap and that felt great. I would say I had some highs and lows today, and I didn't do much to manage that. But I was conscious about what was going on and the more I'm practicing, the more I'm exercising the muscle that switches from a negative thought to a positive one. Actually, it's not so much from negative to positive, but to a higher vibration.

I interviewed an author today on avatars after watching and loving the movie *Avatar*. He spoke of higher dimensional beings and that really brought me into the flow. I feel like I've absorbed a lot of information, and so, all in all, looking back, it has been a good day.

January 25th

INTENTION

I wrote in my journal: "My intention is to welcome abundance, knowledge, ideas, money, joy, happiness, love, wisdom, freedom, gratitude, peace in my life, and people around me that are in contact with me. I open my arms and receive it." Later I went to the gym and while working out, new ideas started flowing.

SHIFTING SELF-DOUBTS

It is 9:21 pm and I'm uploading more videos. Yet, I can feel self doubts creeping in. You know how it is! They just crawl in and try to tell you how unworthy you are and how incapable you are of reaching your dreams. I have those thoughts right now. I just like to switch them off and remind myself that there are plenty of options, and that I am worthy of all the greatness and abundance of this world, and my thoughts are creating my reality. I just have to step up and open up for greatness to show up and manifest!

LIVE OUT TRUTH

As James Redfield, author of *The Celestine Prophecy* said when I interviewed him, *"The most important thing is for us to live in our truth."* I've noticed that doing so actually results in a much more human, harmonious, and loving conversation because I am saying what is true. I am not speaking with an objective in my mind, not manipulating, but rather, just being authentic in the conversation and in my own life.

Like so many people, I have been hurt in the past and as a result, I've built a really thick wall around me. Now, with so many things coming into my life, so many opportunities, I have to constantly step up. And in order to step up, I have to move beyond that wall and open up. The more I'm doing that, the more I think amazing opportunities are going to be created in my life.

January 26th

GRATEFUL TO BE ALIVE NOW

It's nearly 10:30 am. I am thrilled to be here on this planet. I'm very grateful to be alive during this evolution in the world, to be a witness, and to participate in what is currently happening. I feel that what will be unfolding in the next 15 years will be a tremendous shift for us all.

TEAM WORK

I received great news as I was interviewing Patrice Percie du Sert on the pollen and bee therapy for LaNutrition.fr. I got an email from Japan, and they have accepted my book offer! How cool is that?

So, I'm excited and grateful to have Sabine handling the international copyright contracts for me, instead of doing them myself. I now feel more relaxed about involving people that are specialists in their domains with my work. A few years ago, even a few months ago, I wouldn't have wanted any intermediaries, as I thought I could do it all on my own. While I have learned a lot by doing many things myself, I can't be everywhere at once, so when I was not allowing others to help me, I think I was limiting my success. I'm very excited to have my book in Japanese! I'm so, so thankful.

HOW TO DEFINE ABUNDANCE?

I think it's important to let go of expectations, let things happen, feel Universal energy, and listen to Divine guidance. But how do we define abundance? How can we measure it? When do we become abundant? For now, I'm opening myself up to the beautiful, loving abundance that creates even more opening of the heart and magnificence in every single way. I want to take the time to work further on what abundance means in different areas of my life.

SPIRITUAL ABUNDANCE

As far as spiritual abundance, I define it as ongoing growth, learning, opening up, and yes, spiritual growth. I would also like to learn how to share in new ways and be in tune with Universal wisdom. I want to be a vessel for helping to communicate Universal wisdom to others. I envision an abundance of teachers and practices; people with infinite wisdom, high vibration, and pure heart coming to me for interviews. I want to feature and interview an abundance of people that have this knowledge, apply it, have an open heart, and communicate from their entire being and spirit for the best of humankind and evolution.

FINANCIAL ABUNDANCE

Financial abundance for me is to be at peace with money and not worry about having enough. It would mean being able to afford to give myself and those I love whatever I wish to give them, whenever I wish to do so; gifts such as healthy foods, massages, natural healing products, or luxurious, nurturing holidays in amazing places all over the world. It would also mean having a welcoming, cozy home, including a stable for horses; a place where I could relax and host dinners, weekends and retreats with family, friends, and co-creators from all around the world. It would mean being able to spoil loved ones, supporting them in their dreams. It would also mean finally being able to create a foundation that supports thousands of kids each year to travel at a young age so they can discover new cultures and be the great leaders of tomorrow.

ABUNDANCE AT WORK

Abundance at work for me is co-creating with gifted, passionate, and talented individuals. It means having a harmonious and fun team of talented people supporting my vision and having grateful clients. It would mean having free time for myself and my family. It would also mean having the flexibility to travel and explore awesome places around the world and having the opportunity to interview captivating people. It would mean having an international TV show and a production company that provides timely information and juicy content to different media outlets. It would mean having my books translated into many different languages. I also see abundance at work as having unlimited ideas and projects that are aligned with the Universal needs on the planet and, through those projects, helping people grow and further open their hearts. And because I love technology (I'm a big fan of Macs), abundance at work for me also means having available to me an amazing computer system and high-tech toys; powerful tools that would make it possible for me to work even more efficiently and deliver my ideas through quality videos.

ABUNDANCE OF TIME

Abundance of time for me would include having quality time with my friends and family. It would mean being surrounded and bonding with great, beautiful, loving people with an open heart. I see an abundance of time as being limitless and expandable; the Universe providing all the time needed for what is important, real, and fulfilling. It would mean having the time to play sports, travel, be with those I care about, interview amazing people, love, and grow. I see abundance of time as living in the present moment and reminding myself every day how precious life is and how grateful I am to be here now.

ABUNDANCE OF LOVE

Abundance of love to me is about unconditional acceptance, support, and an abundance of meaningful connections. It is about being aligned with networks that allow me to go even further in my dreams and help even more people. I see an abundance of love as being present each and every day and being guided in everything I do; to feel unlimited Divine love flowing through me and from all realms. To me it also means to love and embrace my life and know that Life loves and embraces me in return. To find a loving, pure, shining life partner that shares my passion for making a difference in this World and feeling blessed every day.

CALLING ABUNDANCE

There is unlimited abundance in this Universe in every form you can imagine. I'm calling forth this abundance right now. It is available to all of us, and I'm getting clearer about the fact that we are what we experience in our lives; our experiences are a mirror of who we are. So if we feel abundant, then we are going to manifest abundance. We are abundance. I am going to do a video about all of this right now. Sending you love.

EFFORTLESSLY CREATING WEB TV

It's now 2:43 pm on Tuesday. I have found a great company that offers an online tool to create web TV. It absolutely amazes me what this company has made available. I just sent them a personal acknowledgement to express my appreciation. Sending messages like that is not something people often do in France, but I felt really inspired to congratulate and thank the company.

I have wanted to do web TV for a long time to classify my hundreds of YouTube videos, but it never felt like it was the right moment or like I had the right tools to do it. Now I feel that everything is in perfect alignment. It feels synchronistic and natural to me and, therefore, makes perfect sense for me to move forward. This company was so easy to find and easy to use. They have great online marketing tools and provided everything I needed to make my web TV a success on all levels. For me, this meant easy to find, easy to navigate, and capable of generating new traffic. It is also about having an abundance of information that is simple to share, comment on, and talk about. It creates such a relief. I also love how many videos are posted on my Twitter account (www.twitter.com/liloumace) and on my Facebook account (www.facebook.com/LilouMacewebTV) as soon as they are posted on my web TV. I can easily place an embed video from YouTube or Dailymotion in it.

YOUTUBE VERSUS WEB TV

I was able to set up my web TV really quickly. Now I'm able to generate additional traffic that I wasn't generating through YouTube. Now I can direct people to my own website, and it's even easier to find a video. It's all for free on www.LilouMace.com, and there is information there both in French and in English. I am now receiving traffic to the website instead of only attracting viewers to the videos I post on my YouTube channel (www.Youtube.com/liloumace), where there are a countless number of other videos posted by other people. By choosing to visit my website, viewers now have the option to focus exclusively on the videos that I have created. Also, since the videos are arranged by theme, I think it is a much better system. Actually, there are many reasons to have the website. It makes a lot of sense, and I love it! In the future, I believe many individuals and companies will have their own web TV. YouTube has opened many doors for communicating via videos, and web TV is one of those natural evolutions. I feel that I am in the flow and perfectly aligned with what is needed right now.

WORKING AS A TEAM

I want to take the initiative to welcome more people into the work I am doing and grow a positive, supportive team. I know how to recognize talent in others. Especially now, there are so many people looking for a job who are talented and deserving of recognition. It is like Sabine, my book agent, handling the contract on my behalf right now with the Japanese market. Because she has the talent and has stepped up to take care of that for me, I don't have to worry about it and am free to do other things.

OUR SOUL'S EVOLUTION

We have to fully utilize what we are given, whether it's a hard luck story, a strange background, problems with our parents, financial issues, being born in a ghetto, or being born in a rich family. Wherever we are coming from, what matters is what we learn from that experience. We have to ask ourselves why we incarnated ourselves with that particular set of values, issues, family, worth, poverty and what we are going to do from that starting point? Posing that question gives us quite a lot of clues as to where our purpose lies and how we can attract abundance and be truly fulfilled in this life. I believe that our soul has chosen these lives and surrounded us with these people and these experiences to help us grown, learn, heal, and re-open our hearts to living up to our highest and brightest potential.

LEADING ME TO JOURNALING

I was born in the US to hard-working French parents who definitely loved to travel. I am an only child without brothers or sisters. In time, after my parents and I returned to France, my parents got divorced, and I felt a big betrayal there. My parents' divorce triggered many changes in my life. The experience led me to do a lot of introspective thinking and to do a lot of work on myself as a person. I went through many painful moments and, as a result, I did a lot of questioning about life. Looking back, all of those experiences were perfectly aligned with what I'm now doing in my life. For example, I am able to share these thoughts with you today because I have faithfully kept journals for a very long time. The first time I can remember my journaling having a significant impact was back when I was eight years old, and now I am 32. So, it has been quite a long time for me.

There are no coincidences. That is something I particularly realized during the period of time when I turned my journaling habit and passion into my first book. Keeping track of my life experiences is what my videos are about and that is part of my life purpose. I do love sharing and, when I look back, everything points to that. Clearly, my unique way of authentically expressing myself is my strength, and that's what I focus on because it is what I love doing. It is also the special blessing that comes from my life experiences. My life is shaped and informed by my soul's story.

I think that our potential expands once we are grateful for our past and can turn our experiences into something amazing that will show us how to help, bond, and be there for others. In any type of business, that's what is really needed and what it means to be a true success.

January 27th

ASKING FOR GUIDANCE

I ask for guidance from my angels, my guides, and from all time-space reality to provide abundance in my life in ways that I'm not even able to conceive of right now and to bring that manifestation into my life now, magically and effortlessly.

I welcome financial and all other forms of abundance into my life that will provide me with the means to expand on my practices, on the work I am doing to help even more people, and to give me the freedom to travel in order to personally conduct interviews around the world. I want to make an abundant living helping millions of souls. I welcome the guidance and the abundance that will enable me to continue the work I am doing and fulfill my vision.

THE HIDDEN MESSAGES OF WATER

Have you ever read the incredible book written by Dr. Emoto called *The Hidden Messages in Water*? I have read it and found it fascinating. Dr. Emoto is a Japanese scientist who studies how the messages that arise from different emotions can affect crystals of water. In his research, he has exposed water to beautiful melodies, to the word LOVE, or to prayers, and it has resulted in magnificent crystalline patterns forming in the water. In comparison, the water crystals that he exposed to hateful messages resulted in strange, malformed patterns. Through his experiments, he proved to the world that the power of love and gratitude, as well as its opposite emotions, have a unique energy. Since the human body is made up of 70% water, you can imagine what it does to our body when we have negative thoughts.

PRODUCTIVE DOING NOTHING

It's 4:40 pm and for the past hour, I've been wondering what to do. There's nothing I really want to do or feel like doing, but it's not because of laziness. I just don't know what to do. I'm just going to relax, enjoy the stillness and peace. Doing something for the sake of being busy is useless in many ways. It won't move you forward. Only inspired actions lead to fulfilling results. They create magic, synchronicity, ease, and play. For me this is the only way of being now. I remind myself of this when I become afraid and feel the urge to do, do, do. It's not that I'm in a negative mood; it's just that I feel like doing nothing.

I've spent an hour or two in front of the computer this afternoon and, frankly, there's nothing for me to do, and it's rare for me to say that. Usually I'm super busy and running left and right. But at the moment, I can't see anything useful to do; no major and inspired action steps to take.

So, co-creator, I'm either going to meditate, grab a book, or just relax. It's a lovely day out. I could go for a walk in nature. I feel it is more productive to do that sort of thing rather than just sitting in front of a computer for hours for no special reason.

Yesterday, I was on the computer uploading an interview until midnight. I have this kind of non-linear schedule. I could pre-set a schedule, but sometimes I like working at night and not during the day. So, for now, I'm going to make myself a little cup of green tea and follow the next inspired steps I am led to take. I'm waiting on the next synchronicity. ;)

MOVING BEYOND SHYNESS

It's 8:30 pm. I have just watched two of my favorite shows here in France: *C à vous* and *Fourchette et sac à dos*. Both are hosted by great, bubbly hostesses. I observe the hostesses to learn from them. I just have tears of joy and sadness in my eyes, mixed emotions, when I see how eloquent they are. I have great admiration for their communication skills. I know that I have good questions in my mind when I'm interviewing people, but sometimes I have a hard time clearly formulating the questions, presenting topics, and speaking with other people around. I begin thinking, *"I can't do this."* I sometimes wonder why I am so attracted to the sort of work I do! It is like a stronger force is behind me and has attracted me to it. I cannot resist doing it, and I love it. Yet, at times, it feels so difficult. I think for me, it is just a matter of becoming more confident. I have natural qualities that are a great match to my work, but overcoming my shyness, my fear of doing something wrong, or not being good enough is a big challenge for me. Once I become more confident, I know that I will move forward professionally and rise to a whole new level.

THE PAINFUL LONGING OF A CLEAR VISION

I'm bursting into tears. I have just so much longing and wanting to do the work I am inspired to do. I have promised myself that one day I will be able to overcome my fears and learn what I must learn so I can do some extraordinary things.

My dream is to one day have my own TV show that combines travel and spirituality. In that show, I would attend spiritual leaders' workshops, interview the teachers, and then share my experience and insights on camera. I would do this in many different cultures around the world. I would show that we are all one; we are all the same, beyond what seem to be our "differences." We are all looking for the same thing: to experience love.

I can so clearly see my vision. It brings me so much joy that it is nearly painful. It's a mix of emotions. I can see it so close; it is right in front of me and yet at the same time, it is still so far away. I have such a strong, strong, strong desire to do this, such a profound longing that, at times, it is almost terrifying.

January 29th

AN UNEXPECTED CALL

It's 7:00 pm. Oh my gracious God, Infinite Power and Source! I am so excited! I was reading *The Fifth Agreement* by Don Miguel Ruiz, a book that I just received today, and I'm enjoying the fact I'll be interviewing this amazing teacher on the 5th of February. I was just reading about symbolism and how we see reality a certain way because of how we've been taught and the version of life we've inherited and—just at that moment—my cell phone rang. You won't guess who it was! Oh, I'm excited. I'm so excited. It was Guy Trédaniel.

A FRENCH PUBLISHER FOR MY BOOK

Guy Trédaniel wants to publish my book in French. Oh my God! Oh! Don Miguel Ruiz has also had his book published there as well as Neale Donald Walsch and Deepak Chopra who are other huge names in the spiritual realm. So I am really excited, co-creator. You're the first one to hear this. Oh my God. Oh my God. Oh my God. This is so awesome. Guy said, *"Please email me with the dates that you can meet me in Paris. We'll discuss this."* As you can imagine, my beautiful co-creators, angels of light, this is as good as it gets. How juicy is that?! I'm so excited. Ok. Ok. Ok.

ONE THING BRINGING ANOTHER

While I was in the flow, I also advised Guy to set up a web TV channel. I think it would be a wonderful promotional tool for publishers. He said, *"Yeah, I agree with you because there's so much potential. I saw one of our authors, Neal Donald Walsch, last time he was in Paris and there were 2,000 people there and they wanted more."* So I replied, *"Yeah, we've got to give that to them. Video is a great way to feature authors and their books, to share their knowledge, and to get the word out about their books and everything else that they are doing."* Tredaniel Editions has the top spiritual authors in France. People like Deepak Chopra, Debbie Ford, Neal Donald Walsh, Dr. Emoto, Doreen Virtue, and Wayne Dyer all have their books translated into French with this publisher. I would love to interview all those people for Tredaniel Editions' web TV channel! How cool would that be?!

So, this is super, super, super juicy. Oh my God. So I'm going to meet Guy Trédaniel next week or the week following. But having him call me personally is such an honor. He decided to go for it. How cool is that? I received a call from Guy Trédaniel. Wow, I'm going to call my mom now and tell her. How cool…how very cool.

January 30th

TIME FOR A SECOND BOOK

It's 9:11 am, co-creator. I woke up feeling so blessed. I haven't had breakfast yet. I'm going to have a healthy breakfast of whole wheat crepes, but for now I was just looking at my Facebook page. I received a message from Irene Grace. She says, *"Lilou, I am a fan. It's time for another book. Get yourself writing your next book. You have set the enthusiasm and created a following from the first one. It's time to bank on that foundation and keep the spark flying. That's all and more power to you, Lilou. Irene."*

A MESSAGE FROM THE UNIVERSE

I'm so touched and moved by her message. That went straight to my heart. Her first name, Irene, is also the first name of my mom and with her last name being Grace, it feels like I have received a message from the Universe.

I feel that the more we open up, the more we are vulnerable; the more people can contribute to our life and be of support. It is this type of message that gives you the power and the energy of tens and thousands of people. It uplifts you. It reminds me why I'm doing this.

It is indeed like a Divine spirit is speaking through Irene because she's reflecting back the energy that is emanating from my heart. I am sharing this with you as it is happening.

A HEALING CONTRACT

My heart is also so grateful for the call yesterday from Guy Trédaniel. I'm very thankful and grateful for many reasons. I received so many rejection letters from publishing companies that this feels that much more healing and amazing.
I feel really, really connected right now because everything about this publishing company is so right on. I really love their authors. Some people really have a beautiful heart, and I can see that this company has a heart and soul. I love the fact that the owner of the publishing company is calling me himself and wants to meet. I'm very, very happy to be part of their group. I feel it's already like a family. So anyway, now I'm going to have a nice, juicy, healthy breakfast!

SUPPORTIVE NOTES

I find it interesting, the ripple effect that someone encouraging you has in the world. Just the one message I received from Irene inspired me to give back and to encourage someone that gave me inspiration. Next thing I know, I have also received a Facebook message from Jean Dayton letting me know about her Facebook fan page. She is a British artist. I love her art. Unfortunately, I haven't been able to buy any of her work, even though I think it is very affordable. She is truly gifted and I replied to her Facebook message by saying, *"I love your work, Jean. Keep going. You will be highly successful, I know it. You are so on track. Sending you love, Lilou."*

I was inspired to send Jean this message, as Irene did for me. I wanted to remind Jean who she really is and how she's on track. She is participating in the 100-Day Reality Challenge and supporting a lot of other members in that group. She's giving herself through her art. I know she's had some hard times, but I also know she will succeed. My heart tells me so. Sometimes all we need is a supportive note from someone.

A HEART PROCESS

If you're reading this right now, there might be some people who need your help. You don't even need to think about it. They'll just come in your life and your heart will know what to say. On this planet, it's no longer an intellectual process; it's a heart process. The more you open your heart, the more you become vulnerable. The more you express your love and share your gratitude with authenticity, the more it's going to ripple and unfold in a magical way for all of us. We're all one.

YOUR LOVE IS NEEDED ON THIS PLANET

Irene's message had an impact on me, which then had an impact on Jean, who is then going to have an impact on others. Do you see this beautiful flow? Yes, that's the natural flow of life and even when something like Irene sending me a message might seem insignificant by itself, it's actually huge. The power of that one message led to another and to another and who knows which message will touch and change somebody's life? Who knows which message is going to provide that one juicy ounce of encouragement and energy in somebody's life that is going to create a dynamo within them; that is going to shift or maybe even save a life? So, co-creator, please open your heart, don't hold back any longer. Open your heart authentically with integrity and compassion. Your love is needed on this planet.

HEALING POWER OF NATURE

Today it is Saturday and my mom and I went for a two-hour walk in the woods. There's a large wooded area just outside where we live. Even though it was very muddy, the sun was shining and we had such a beautiful time. Actually, right now, it is half snowing and half raining, so I feel very grateful that we went walking. I can remember only a few months ago in the summer when I was here and even in October when I came back to France, I went through so many fears and emotions. Back then, I spent a lot of time in the woods crying and digging deep inside of me. I went through so much anxiety and even had some panic attacks. When you have moments like that, I think you just have to let it out. At the time it felt like an eternity. It felt like that fear would never go away, and yet I moved on.

I'm really grateful that I had nature around me and I took the time to really deal with my fears. I remember one day, standing in the woods, opening my arms, and asking the trees and all of nature to give me their love because I was so empty inside, and I felt so fearful. I could immediately feel nature's love flowing back to me. I talked directly to nature that day, asking for its support, and it gave me an answer. I remember a moment of ecstasy when I was feeling so much energy flowing in. I want to encourage you, when you have difficult moments, to go through them because some amazing things come out of suffering. When it finally comes out, it feels playful yet freeing. The clarity that I have right now in my life, the gratitude and the joy, is much greater than it has ever been before.

KILLING THE DREAM

Looking back over my life, questioning it, was hard. I felt the fears and brought them into my heart, transforming them. I'm grateful that I went through that phase, really grateful. I'm clear that, without doing that healing work, I wouldn't be where I am today. Now I am able to live with my mom, share a great relationship with her, and go fully for my dreams in a healthy environment. Before that, I would have qualified my situation as a dream killer. But instead of outside forces holding me back as I sometimes believed, I was the one killing the dream.

WHAT DO YOU CHOOSE?

It's interesting how our lives and the people around us are mirrors of ourselves. The behavior of those in your life reflects what you have inside; your thoughts and what's really going on. So it's important to take responsibility for our lives. It doesn't have to be something heavy or significant, it can be something simple, but you can begin a great journey right now. Whether you are choosing a vanilla or chocolate flavored life, just choose! Even when it doesn't appear that way, every single moment, choices are available to us. Every single moment we can choose to transform our reality, see things differently, and turn something that seems bad into something good...or the reverse. It's all a matter of perception. In everything there is good. In everything there is bad. Which do you choose?

January 31st

INVICTUS

It is the last day of January, and I just posted a blog. I was looking for the poem *Invictus* by the English poet, William Ernest Henley (1849–1903). The movie by that name tells the story of Nelson Mandela's life. It focuses on the part of his journey in which rugby played a major role in reuniting his country and in the communion of blacks and whites. Here is the poem I posted because I found it so inspiring:

INVICTUS

Out of the night that covers me,
Black as the pit from pole to pole,
I thank whatever gods may be
For my unconquerable soul.
In the fell clutch of circumstance
I have not winced nor cried aloud.
Under the bludgeonings of chance
My head is bloody, but unbowed.
Beyond this place of wrath and tears
Looms but the Horror of the shade,
And yet the menace of the years
Finds and shall find me unafraid.

It matters not how strait the gate,

How charged with punishment the scroll,

I am the master of my fate:

I am the captain of my soul.

I AM THE CAPTAIN OF MY SOUL

I love that line. So that the words will sink in, I keep repeating it out loud to myself: *"I am the captain of my soul."* I went to see this inspiring movie this week, and I wanted to share it with you, co-creator. I hope you're having a beautiful day.

February 4th

NOT GETTING STOPPED

I got apprehensive before interviewing today. I have this apprehension when I haven't been interviewing for a few days. It's like I have never interviewed before. Yet, when I get started, then boom, all fears disappear. I think we all have experiences like that. It's quite normal. But it's important not to get stopped by those feelings. It doesn't mean we're not ready. I have even noticed that if I do not feel this way before an interview and instead I'm over-confident, then the interview does not turn out as well. Actors, for example, when they go on stage, they feel butterflies in their tummy.

A JUICY LIFE

I'm co-creating right now that tomorrow will be a blessed day, a beautiful day, and in the heart. I even did a drawing on my agenda for tomorrow at the top of the page: a heart with rays of light shining out. That's the focus. That's the symbol for tomorrow. I think that's where true abundance resides—when we live in the heart, allow our heart to speak, allow it to freely accept in the moment what is. This includes who we are, who we are not, who other people are, and who they are not. When we are just emanating this love, this unconditional beingness, this awareness of who we are, then our life is juicy. Where the abundance is, that's where the beauty of this world is, and I look forward to experiencing that even more. I'm sharing this with you as it unfolds, as it manifests, and as I take action. There are very few steps to take, because it just happens naturally. It is not an intellectual process; it is a process of the heart. The idea is to fully live in the heart every day and be appreciative of what we have, of the abundance that exists in our world, and to, therefore, attract even more. But honestly, when the heart is open, you feel satisfied right in the moment and you need nothing else. So how do we get to that place, and how can we be at that place all the time? That's a question that I'm raising right now and that I want to look at more closely. I send you a big kiss, co-creator. Now it's time for sleep.

February 5th

WHAT MESSENGER ARE YOU?

It's quite late now. I have done some wonderful interviews today with Angelina Heart on twin flames and on masculine-feminine energy. It was a very interesting interview. I followed that by interviewing Don Miguel Ruiz, bestselling author of *The Fifth Agreement*. He is just such a loving soul. By just looking into his eyes, oh my God, you're in love. It was an absolutely magnificent and life-changing interview. At one point, he said that each of us is a messenger, whether we are conscious of it or not. The question is: What messenger are you? We are given the gift of this precious life, so what message do we convey through our way of being in this world and what we say to those around us?

I think Don Miguel Ruiz is wonderful. He is coming from the heart and has such a beautiful spirit. He said that we are all messengers; we're angels here on this planet. So, what kind of message are we giving ourselves? This is such a key and the core of a life changing perspective!

I'm a messenger, just as you are, and by sharing our lives with others, we make a difference in their lives as well. So what kind of message are you going to share? Mine is a message of inspiration and joy, of freedom and empowerment, of love, growth, and gratitude. I am redefining those messages every day, but I definitely want to show that there is a different way of seeing life and there are different things we can manifest, experience, and allow.

I'm really, really grateful to have met Don Miguel Ruiz and to have had the opportunity to interview him. He is very talkative and just such a loving man. I had prepared so many questions, but he was just unfolding it all. It was very beautiful. I look forward to interviewing his son, Don Jose Ruiz, next week. Don Jose also co-wrote the book.

Well, it's bed time now. I send you much love, co-creator. I'll be doing my little gratitude list just before going to bed and closing my eyes. Then I will wake up tomorrow morning
in love with life.

NO LIMITATIONS

I feel very blessed to share these messages. Viewers on YouTube have asked me: How are you posting so many videos online? How are you doing them? How many assistants do you have? Frankly, I'm doing all this by myself but, obviously, right now it's midnight and I'm still on the computer!

When you love doing something, time does not exist! I must say that even if I were homeless, I would still be grabbing my camera and interviewing people on the street and finding a way to upload videos! I see no boundaries and no limitations.

February 9th

THE UNIVERSE GIVES BACK

It's now 8:00 pm. I'm back home and checking my emails. I received wonderful news from Regis who has been helping me in many different ways, including video editing. He just received a big screen television as a gift from a company for whom he helped create a DVD. He told me, *"I feel so blessed because I wasn't expecting this and it is amazing how the Universe rewards us in such magnificent and beautiful ways."* Regis is truly a person who is unselfishly of service to others. He is an example of how someone can attract so many different things in so many different ways. He has received everything from a car to a computer to a television to an iPhone. All different forms of abundance come to him as a consequence of the authentic person he is in this World. I thank him for being such an understanding, loving spirit, for expressing those gifts unconditionally, and for sharing that information with others. I look forward to doing more camera, montage, technical, and editing work with him. He is very inspiring.

FLYING ON OUR OWN

As much as I have been seeing myself through Oprah for such a long time, I now feel that I have reached a place in my life where, instead of constantly comparing myself to her, I can feel proud of what I am achieving and doing on my own. Making this shift is very freeing. I think role models are uplifting to a point, but then you need to detach and develop as an individual. It feels as if I have finally found my wings. I am growing and it is now possible for me to fly on my own. Oprah still exists for me, but now I am more in touch with myself. I am enjoying the ride and feeling very grateful.

FEELING THE ABUNDANCE

I have received the confirmation that I will be meeting with Guy Trédaniel and Ben Jafari. Guy is the owner and Ben is the commercial director of a big publisher of spiritual books in France. I'll be meeting them in Paris next week. I feel so grateful, co-creator. I can't begin to express how open my heart is. I find myself in such a beautiful place. I feel the abundance. It is unfolding and I am ready to receive.

February 11th

THE INNER MIRROR

I love the number 11, so when I saw that it was February 11th; I knew that this had to be an exciting day, right? Ha ha. It is so amazing how everything we experience is a mirror of how we are feeling inside. There actually is no such thing as outside. Everything is happening inside of us. It's really wild. I just had an interesting day; some great interviews and some quiet time. I was feeling on the easy going side this morning. When I woke up, I looked at myself in the mirror and said, *"You are prosperous. You deserve greatness. You deserve to be compensated financially and lovingly for all the effort and the great energy you put out there."*

HO'OPONOPONO

I was listening to what author and inspirational speaker Dr. Joe Vitale was saying. He was explaining how, at a time in his life when he was homeless, he came across *Ho'oponopono*, a book written by an elderly Hawaiian therapist by the name of Dr. Ihaleakala Hew Len. Along with Dr. Hew Len, Dr. Vitale later wrote a very interesting book called *Zero Limits*. It is about forgiving yourself, humanity, and the whole world to a degree, for anything that is happening in your life whether you think you have created it or not. This ancient technique, which has its origins in Hawaii, apparently has had amazing results and has been used successfully by many people around the world. This is one way of viewing Ho'oponopono of many different interpretations. It is not the only one! But I feel the truth of it.

FORGIVING VERSUS CANCELING

I am drawn to reading Dr. Vitale's book. After reading only the first few paragraphs, I began to apply some of the practices today. For example, before when I would have negative thoughts about money, I would focus on canceling those thoughts. Now, instead of simply canceling, I am also forgiving myself for thinking those thoughts. I prefer including forgiveness as I feel it creates a clearing on many levels. Once we forgive, we can create something else from there. So as soon as I have those money beliefs, I say to myself, *"I forgive myself for thinking in this limiting way, and I am now creating abundance in every sense of the term."*

February 12th

HUMBLING EXPERIENCE OF LIVING AT MY MOTHER'S

I must say that I am ashamed to currently be living at my mother's house. I'm 32 years old and, even though I try to convince myself that it's alright, I'm still not comfortable when people ask me where I live. I want to go beyond that, and I want to clear that up because, yes, the truth is at this point I can't afford to live anywhere else on my own. To fully recognize that fact is very humbling. This is the reality. This is what's happening. I think it is essential that I not add any drama to that fact, but simply accept it at face value.

BEATING MYSELF UP

I have a tendency to beat myself up about things. I can be really hard on myself. That's what I did about my weight issues. That's also what I did about my money issues. Whenever I find myself in a tough situation, I end up having a mean conversation with myself to get back up. Unfortunately, a lot of us do that, and that's definitely not a healthy way to deal with what is happening in our lives. So my intention now is to apply the *Ho'oponopono* technique. Instead of being angry and hateful with myself, I will face my situation by being forgiving and clearing the energy by saying to myself, *"Listen, that's okay."*

DOING THE RIGHT THING WHETHER I WAS HOMELESS OR NOT

I forgive myself for not being self-sufficient at the moment and not earning an abundant living by doing the work I love. Because

I am doing what I love, my life is perfect as it is right now. I'm very, very grateful to have a roof over my head, to have a car I can borrow when I need to drive somewhere. Doing what I love is so essential in my life that I would do it whether I was homeless or not. I am aspiring for more and, at the same time, I am grateful for what I have now.

SHIFTING THE VIBRATION WITH MUSIC

As I am driving, a Michael Bublé song comes on the radio. He is singing "I Just Haven't Met You Yet." Ah, I love that song. I love Michael Bublé. He's so big right now in France, and this just reminds me of my best friend Daniel. Many years ago, when we were living in Miami, he's the one who made me aware of Michael Bublé. I just love that Michael Bublé is so popular in France that I can hear him on the radio through the Energy, NRG station. Wow, that's amazing. The energy of that song just lifts you up, doesn't it? Music is such a powerful tool when you want to shift your energy. Just put on your favorite song, or hear it on the radio, and it's just like—boom—instantly your spirits fly straight through the roof. Yeah, baby!!!!

BLOSSOMING RELATIONSHIP WITH MOM

It is time to go to bed now. I'm quite excited about all the wonderful possibilities in my life. I'm grateful for today. I am grateful for all the beautiful conversations and synchronicities that are unfolding. I give thanks and look forward to tomorrow.

The next two evenings I will be helping my mom at her restaurant. She has a Mexican restaurant in Nantes and, since it is Valentine's Day, there are going to be a lot of people coming out for a meal. I look forward to spending that time with her. I love how our relationship has improved. There is just so much love now present and expressed. I'm so grateful for this opportunity to be close to her. I think it was very much needed and part of a healing process for both of us. I know it is important to just allow the process to unfold naturally. It has already manifested on so many levels. I am also so thankful to be sharing all this with you and hopefully inspiring you in your own life.

February 13th

TECHNOLOGY TO CONNECT AND SERVE MORE

Today is Saturday. It's 1:11 pm. I know I'm attracting 11 all the time. I am so on track! I'm uploading some videos and backing up my iPhone. I am stepping out of my comfort zone because I'm not all that technical, but recently I've learned how to be a little more technical. I know that technology serves me in reaching even more people so, in that regard, it is definitely a great thing.

SHINING OUT

This morning I looked at some of the comments on my YouTube page (youtube.com/liloumace), and there was a note from one of my subscribers that said, *"Oh my God. I just watched some of your videos from over three years ago in 2006 and it's amazing to see where you were back then and where you're at now. You're glowing now and it's so wonderful..."* That comment inspires me to continue on this path. I feel very connected. I'm going to practice sending love and intensifying that love by giving it some special attention right now. I feel blessed.

TRANSCENDING TIME

My co-creator, I hope you are opening your heart too right now and feeling the energy of the words on these pages, even if you are actually reading them months or years later. This is how time and reality is transcendent. I feel your energy right now. I feel your love. And this gives me tremendous support. In return, I send you all my support and love and light so you can find your purpose and follow your passion. You already know what you are here to do. It is something you have enjoyed doing all your life. It is what you are good at, because it comes naturally to you. It is what you love. You might not be great at it yet, but you love it unconditionally and the potential for greatness is inside you at this very moment. This is it, my beautiful co-creator. It is just that simple.

February 15th

IS GOD NOTHING BUT LOVE?

In the morning, I was intensifying the love vibration around me and being in love with life when I received an email from Keya. She wrote to tell me that she had seen my interview with Angelina Heart on the subject of twin flames and sent me a link saying, *"Check out my music."*

I receive a lot of emails with links to a variety of things, and I don't always click on them. But this time, I did click on the link Keya provided, and I found some beautiful songs. I think she is very talented. At the end of the first song, there was the line: *"And they haven't got that God is nothing but love."* That line really hit me and led me to ask myself the question: *"Is God nothing but love?"*

To share my own personal breakthrough, I posted a video last night on this subject. Since I started opening my heart, I have been feeling love again; letting it in and sending it out. And when I heard the line: *"God is nothing but love,"* all of a sudden, I felt God fully in all dimensions. As I said in the video, for the longest time, God was a word that I rarely used or wanted to get close to because even the word scared me.

GOD IS EVERYWHERE

Regarding this subject, I know that I have a long way to go and many more things to work on, but I have made a start. In fact, I think we all know that it's not really about doing a lot of hard work on things, it's just about allowing and opening up to new understandings. So I'm opening up right now to this love and this abundance because, all of a sudden, I feel present to the fact that we are love. Love is everywhere. If God is nothing else but love, then even if love is intangible, now I feel it, know it, and sense it. I feel God everywhere and in everything. That is a huge awakening because it also means that we are God. We have heard this statement before, but this time it didn't fly over my head; it really sank in. It actually went directly to my heart. I felt the impact. It was quite a shift in reality. It was also perfect timing, because if this information had come to me before my heart was truly open, I know I would not have perceived it the same way.

THE COURAGE TO SHARE

I received a number of responses and many comments to the video I posted online. I'm very happy that I found the courage to share my experience. As soon as you mention the "G word" you know that different things come up for different people. My intention was not to suggest that I now know who God is on this planet. I am not into that sort of thing at all. For me, it is more about feeling the love and how beautiful that is.

IT IS ALL HAPPENING FOR A DEEPER REASON

I'm going to let the Universe do the rest of the job. I don't really have to do anything, you know? This is perfect and I'm really excited.

My bank account is getting a little bit on the dry side right now, but instead of worrying, I am just relaxing and trusting. Being at my mother's is certainly removing some financial pressures. I know deep in my heart that there is another reason why I am here spending time with her. I have been longing to get close to her and to heal wounds from the past. Our relationship has been nurturing, and there is a beautiful harmony between us right now.

IN SYNC WITH YOUR SOUL

I received this wonderful message in an email from a beautiful co-creator. It is entitled "In Sync with Your Soul." I do not know where this piece comes from originally or the name of the author. It reads:

"Love is the most powerful force in the entire Universe. It is the energy that binds and sustains all. It is the force from which the Universe and all life is born. Being in love with the Universe connects one to the spiritual power-lines of the Cosmos. This allows one to feel connected to all of Creation every moment of their lives. Once one is in sync with this power, you become in tune with the Universal Plan. When you are one with the Plan, the Universe is able to send energy and resources your way, in the forms of guidance, knowledge, spiritual wisdom, priceless moments of intense beauty, and protection. The Universe is one living organism, and when you are synchronized with its Divine Plan, the whole organism will work to sustain and help you in your goals, which are in fact its goals. All of Creation recognizes you as a peaceful co- creator and smiles upon you with infinite joy, love, wisdom, and guidance."

February 16th

Tomorrow, I'm off to Paris. I have been asking the Universe to let abundance flow; let it flow. It's a beautiful, sunny day here in France, although it is quite cold at only 1° C. Now I'm going to have lunch in a beautiful restaurant with my mom and her friends. I am really grateful to be having access to all this abundance and taking the time to enjoy this lunch as I am going to be having some busy days over in Paris. But, for the moment, instead of being in a state of "go, go, go," which I usually am, I'm staying a little bit longer. In fact, I am staying over the weekend, which I rarely do. This way, I will have more time to appreciate all the people around me and enjoy the company of my friends. On Friday, I'm going to have a beautiful day full of interviews. It will be a wonderful time, and I will be sharing all the little adventures I will be having here with you. It is exciting!

February 17th

WHAT KIND OF FRIENDS ARE THEY?

It's so important to have loving, supportive friends. Are those you consider friends, people who support you? How do they react when you give them good news? Are they happy for you, or are they jealous of your success? Do they challenge you in a good way, or are they negative and toxic? How do the people in your life express their friendship? How do you feel in their presence? It is important to ask yourself these questions and then listen to the answers.

AN ANGEL FRIEND

Baptist de Pape and I have never met in person, but we are friends.

At this point in my life, I'm closer to Baptist than almost anyone in my life. We communicate on a regular basis. We've been doing that for nine months now. Baptist was able to help me because he was there at the right time. He was such an important person for me when I went through intense panic attacks brought on by my fear of running out of money. I was able to let him know what was really going on with me, even when I could not bring myself to tell others. He was there for me with understanding, wisdom, and compassion. His gentle spirit just opened me up so much. I'm very thankful for our friendship, which has been very healing and nurturing.

In this world, I consider Baptist not only a friend, but an angel. He is just there for me with kindness, asking for absolutely nothing in return.

I am leaving for Paris tonight, and I have an amazing day ahead tomorrow. I've been preparing for my interviews with Sylvie Simon and Frédéric Lenoir. All day Friday I'll be interviewing, and Regis Abitbol is helping me. He is an angel with a camera. There are some beautiful things ahead. A lot of synchronicity has been unfolding and I feel very blessed and grateful right now.

February 18th

CREATING INTENTIONS

I'm in Paris and just two minutes away from meeting with editor Guy Trédaniel. I'm creating the intention that it will all flow naturally and effortlessly, and that I will be offered a wonderful proposal for my book. I also want to move forward with doing videos, interviewing all the amazing authors this publisher represents. Let the magic unfold!

APPEALING TO ALL

Hello, beautiful co-creator. Well, I'm in the French underground and just came out of the meeting with Guy Trédaniel. This publisher represents a huge number of international authors. They're very interested in my interviewing them. They are also interested in publishing my book. So it was really a beautiful, abundant meeting where all the synchronicities came together. Among the authors they represent are Eckhart Tolle, Deepak Chopra, and Jerry and Esther Hicks. So the idea of my doing interviews in English with their authors and then adding French subtitles is really appealing to them and to me!

The other great news is that I won't need to translate my book *I Lost My Job and I Liked It* into French. It will be translated by someone I know will do a great job. I'm really very appreciative of this moment. A year after writing my first book, there is a chance it will be bought by a major publisher and translated into French. Not only that, but I may have the opportunity to interview some wonderful spiritual authors. This publisher may also develop their own web TV. If they do that, they will be the first one to do so in France. This is such a privilege and an achievement for me. I am in awe.

CREATING WITH A TEAM

I just received a phone call from Regis. I am very grateful to have him in my life, especially with all the interview requests I've been getting lately. With his help, I can concentrate and focus on doing the interviews, and he does the montages for me—the editing part that I don't enjoy doing. So it is a way to receive, but also to share. Every person has a special gift that brings them joy. Through this work, Regis and I are each doing what we love doing and, in the end, sharing the joy of what we have created together.

February 23rd

UNLOCKING ENERGY

Yes, positive energy is flowing and it is like a conduit to abundance that has opened in my life. I feel really confident moving forward and see really beautiful things ahead. There are just so many different ideas and possibilities coming up.

I don't believe in coincidence, but I have to say that everything is really clicking and coming together in a synchronistic way. It's like something has been unlocked on an energetic level. I cannot explain this, but I am loving it. This has been true on a financial, emotional, and relationship level. It is like all the lines of communication have been cleared at once. I'm really thankful for this. It's like so many new gateways are now open. I wonder if this is all the result of the conversations I have been having? Is the confidence I am feeling coming as a direct result of the enlightened spirits I have been contacting? Is it in response to the communications I have been having with my angels and spirit guides asking them to help me? Or is it the result of my ongoing conversation with my soul group?

I think it is honestly the accumulation of all these things. All I can say is that the sense of connection and flow I am experiencing right now is really amazing. I feel more myself, more on track, and I'm so grateful for this, co-creator. I have been waiting for my life to open up and be in the flow for so very long. Thank you. Thank you. Thank you.

A STRONG WORK ETHIC

In speaking of the work ethic I inherited from the hard-working woman that I chose as a mom in this life, I want to make an important distinction. Growing up, I was taught that you have to work really hard to make money and have a good life in this world. I'm very grateful for the values that taught me, but I now know that it is equally important to understand that you do not achieve success only in proportion to how hard you work, but how deeply you believe in yourself. You achieve it on an energetic level that is measured by how focused you are about living an authentic life. This means being courageous in pursuing your dreams and being open to receiving the many forms of abundance the Universe will send you as a result. I'm so grateful that my mom owns a restaurant. Her hard work made it possible for her to provide me with a wonderful education and for her to live a comfortable life. But she is still working so hard. She's 62 and won't be able to retire any time soon. I now understand that there are many paths a person can choose in this world, and I am pursuing one of my own.

As you know, when I left the UK in October, my mom opened her house to me. It is now the end of February, and I can't believe I've been there that long. But there are so many things happening and so much completion that is needed.

February 24th

MAKING PROGRESS!

It is 8:30 pm co-creator and, two hours ago, I interviewed Layne Dalfen. I also interviewed her back when I was living in the UK from my apartment. I remember we did my very first webcam interview. I was using a system other than Skype at the time, and it wasn't working very well. Still to this day, that video had gotten about 4,000 views. It is clear that a lot of people are interested in decoding dreams and understanding their messages. On some level, I think we are all aware that our unconscious minds deal with many issues during sleep in the form of dreams. So I did a proper Skype interview with Layne this time. But I remember that first interview with her so clearly and vividly. I was so nervous, and I did the interview through Wi-Fi from my bedroom. It helps me see how much progress I've made; even though I felt confident that I was in the flow during that first interview. I can see how much more depth we got into this time.

OPRAH'S PRODUCERS

Layne told me she knows a few Oprah Winfrey producers and has been talking with one of them for the past year. She will send the video of our interview to them. I thought that was very sweet of her. I told her that they have heard about me. I've bugged them so many times. I've even sent emails directly to the producers that I had worked with at the time. They were thinking about featuring the 100-Day Reality Challenge in a show about the Law of Attraction. Eighteen participants were selected to be in the video they were going to feature proving that the Law of Attraction worked. It was such a beautiful experience. But at the very last minute, it didn't work out, and I remember them saying to me, *"Welcome to showbiz."*

So yes, a number of Oprah Winfrey producers have seen me and heard about me, especially when I was living in Chicago. I went to Harpo Studios many times in the hopes of being in the audience for an Oprah show. Sometimes, when it was bad weather, I was able to get in and that was great! I saw her show four times and was able to marinate in the atmosphere, observe her, the cameras, the production team, etc.

TRUE HAPPINESS

We desperately want money because we identify with money as a means of buying things that will make us feel good. I now know that things are only things. They are not the measure of true happiness. The happiness that comes from buying things is a false, temporary happiness. You need to go much deeper within yourself to find genuine and lasting happiness. You need to find what you really love and become grounded before success and true happiness can come to you. Otherwise, you're not going to be able to appreciate it fully when it arrives.

I am not relating to how much money I have because I feel like a millionaire. I feel amazing. I feel unlimited. I feel so abundant. The numbers that represent my bank account are not what are directing my life at this time. My life is not defined by those numbers. My mood is not measured in proportion to those numbers. We are so much more than that, co-creators. I can remember a time my mood was so related to the money thing, and I'd be so scared. But I realize now that it is all about choices. I made a choice. You also have choices to make if you want to remove stress from your life. Of course, I don't want to live at my mother's house for the rest of my life. But, I'm crystal clear right now that I love what I am doing and nothing is more important than that. No matter what my life circumstance, I would still pick up a video camera, interview people, and find a way to upload those videos. Knowing that is what keeps me focused and strong. I am so grateful to be sharing this with you right now, co-creators, because this is the real essence of life and what we all have access to, every last one of us.

February 26th

24 HOURS TO MANIFEST AN HD CAMERA

Guess who just called me? It was someone who very rarely calls. It was my dad. My dad is someone who is not around very often. He's very much into his own space and loves travelling. In fact, the last beautiful moments we shared took place on a river cruise through Holland and Belgium that I had invited him to share with me. As I was responsible for taking care of a group of about 30 travel agents, this whole beautiful cruise was offered to me. I was able to invite a guest, so I took my dad. That was really the first time in quite some time when we bonded again. So now here he is suddenly calling me and saying, *"I'm going to offer you the camera that you said you would like to have and were thinking of getting but you didn't know how. Well, I want to offer that to you."*

Wow! Yesterday I called my dad because I had received an email from Regis, the person who does all the film editing and montage work for me, and in the email Regis had said, *"I'm making a* declaration to the Universe that we will attract the camera we need in some way." And I said, "Yeah, I'm fully with you. Let's attract it. Let's put the declaration out there and it will happen. We don't know how, but it will happen." Shortly after that, I had the inspiration to call my dad and I said to him, "Listen, do you by any chance have a camera that you're not using that I can borrow for my interviews because when I'm traveling and interviewing people in person, I need a good camera." And he said, "No. I'm using the camera I have all the time and it's not that good," and he added, "I used to have a good one." And I asked him, "What did you do with it?"

This led him to telling me a long story about how, when he was crossing France with his donkey (yes, with his donkey), at some point, the donkey stepped on his camera. He was initially able to repair it, but then he went on a trip to some others countries and eventually the camera died for good. So he was explaining all of this to me. I think this is because my dad still had this view of me as being a person who is defined by money. I will admit that in the past that was once true, but it is no longer who I am. Because he is a very spiritual person himself, it always really frustrated him that I was more materialistic. It was the very thing he didn't want me to be.

But in this conversation, he must have sensed something different in me, because I wasn't asking him to buy me a new camera. I was coming from a completely different place. So it was pretty amazing when he called and said, *"I want to offer you this camera."* I'm very, very grateful for his generosity because he is not usually such a giving person. I have just sent an email to Regis letting him know what happened. He's going to be really surprised because only 24 hours have passed between the declaration for the camera and having it manifest.

February 27th

CLAIMING YOUR ABUNDANCE

I'm very much impacted by the interview I did with Kishori Aird regarding the vortex and the zero point. Kishori spoke about how important it is to get to that place of harmony and balance because that creates a powerful force of attraction. Seeing both the good and the bad, and bringing both sides into the light, you then create a convergence point and open up amazing energy. For example, if you have doubts about yourself and you are saying, *"Oh, I can't express myself well"* or *"I'm not good enough"* then other people pick up on that vibration around you. If you don't bring your beliefs into the light and balance them, you don't claim what belongs to you, and somebody else will claim it instead of you.

Many people are not claiming what belongs to them, like job promotions, soul mates, money, or love. So instead of holding yourself back with fear, how about claiming abundance? I'm claiming abundance, co-creator! Are you? Let's see what real abundance is. Are you ready for the ride?

I'm attracting abundance even though I'm not quite sure how it is happening. What is important is creating a zero point, a point of balance and, therefore, a point of attraction. The tornado of abundance will pick up speed from there. Ooh la la! Va va voom!

February 28th

SHARING THIS JOURNEY

I know that sharing this journey is essential for me to realize that living a fulfilled life is our birth right. We can do anything we wish to do in our lives if we apply the knowledge and wisdom that is available to all of us. It doesn't matter where we come from or what our experience is. It's available. It's possible. And so, hopefully, this book will inspire you to believe in the power of your dreams. Right now, it is inspiring me to continue on this journey, to keep opening my heart, to keep opening myself up to receiving. I am relaxing, bringing myself back into the rhythm, and waiting for the next synchronicity.

March 5th

TRUE ABUNDANCE

I have to say that since I started putting together this book, I have been worried that you are going to read examples of some of the money I've attracted and possibly think, *"That is a ridiculously small amount. How can you be excited about that?"* Well, it all depends on your perspective. Being happy to receive $100 may seem strange to people who want to attract millions, but I now understand that it is important to be *grateful* for everything because *that* is where the juice is. It's not about the amount. It does not mean that you're *stuck at that level* if you receive a small amount of money and are thankful for it. What you consider abundance and what I consider abundance may be different. True abundance takes many forms and exists in many areas of our lives.

Of course, it will make a difference when I am able to make a magnificent living from my work, because it is so beautiful to be compensated for doing what you love. Yes, sometimes I'm impatient, but that is when I have to remind myself that what is for my highest good already exists for me, and I don't need to worry. It's just a matter of things manifesting on this plane of reality. It reminds me to just relax, allow things to unfold, and wait on the next synchronicity. Since I love what I'm doing, I am constantly sending out a powerful attraction from the heart. We are all powerful attractors. We are all spiritual magnets. If we put our hearts into it, then our vibration sends ripples out into the Universe, and all we have to do is trust and allow.

March 7th

NONE OF MY BUSINESS

Tomorrow is Monday, and I feel that everything is going to unfold as it should. It's not my business to interfere with the Universe or its timing. I just need to follow. We all need to follow the synchronicities of life. I look forward to the manifestation of all I desire and know that it is already manifesting every day in so many different ways. It's quite obvious to me now. Even though we're human and life has its ups and downs. As Jerry and Esther Hicks say, we're on this planet experiencing contrasts because they help us to be even more grateful for what we have and come to know what we really want. It is part of what we came here to do; to live the life we're supposed to live, once we find the courage to do so. I am convinced that is true, and I think you have also noticed how the Universe aligns itself in such a beautiful way.

LOVE AND ABUNDANCE

I hope this story has provided you with some inspiration. Living it inspires me very much. I'm feeling love inside. Love and abundance are exactly the same. The more we are able to love ourselves, the more abundance we can let into our lives. It's the exact same energy. It's so beautiful. It's that gratitude, that profound love, and that sense of connection that creates everything. So our job is to love ourselves, hold the intention that we will have the best this planet has to offer, and things will just unfold from there. That's what we're here to do. We're here to have a good time, right? I wish you a beautiful night's sleep co-creator, and I'll speak to you tomorrow.

March 10th

HEART INTENTION

I'm about to call the editor of Trédaniel. Yesterday I received the contract for my book, and there are a lot of changes needed that I definitely have to verify. What they have sent to me appears to be a standard contract that has not been adapted to my situation. I'm only selling them the rights to my book in France. I think it's very important for authors to be aware, be wise, and also get the professional support they need before signing anything.

I'm about to talk to them about their web TV and me creating a series of video interviews for them with their authors. I'm setting an intention that they are thrilled with my proposal, want to proceed, and that we will decide together what will be the best number of video interviews. This is a big one for me!

We can get started next week with a deposit of some money from them, and then I can really get going. Once my interviews on behalf of this publisher are online, I can quickly begin contacting other editors, because I can see a lot of interest being generated. This is a milestone for me, so I'm asking for the full support of the Universe. I am declaring that my highest and best self will be present in this conversation. I want my heart to be fully open and to connect deeply on a soul level to co-create this amazing opportunity. First and foremost, I want to spread the authors' important messages so that more and more people in France read these books and, as a result, raise their consciousness. That is my prayer. That is my declaration to the Universe. I also declare that, as a consequence of this manifestation, I will be abundant financially, and there will be many, many more opportunities and prosperity to come that will benefit everyone involved. Now we're talking abundance, co-creator! Woo hoo!

BEING CLEAR

I was really clear on all points, and I'm proud of myself for speaking out and not holding back. It is about knowing who you are and what you are worth; not in an arrogant, detached, or pushy way. It is about being honest and having self confidence. I have to say, this is not the first time I have had a contract discussion. My experience in the US was very useful here, and the attention that I created in advance of the discussion created a powerful context for what followed. At this point, what they really wanted to hear was my commitment to sharing their message and spreading the news.

WE DESERVE TO BE PAID

I would do the interviews anyway, even if I wasn't being paid, because that's what I love. But in this abundant world, we all deserve to be paid for something that we're good at and love doing. Can you tell that I'm excited? Yeah, I'm way too high right now, and I'm going to have to balance it all out with the zero point. This is still work for me, and it can be challenging working with French authors. That being said, I'm a bit more centered now.

So that's abundance, co-creator. To receive this amount of money is really something, and it represents just one editor. It is likely to interest other editors at other publishing companies who would like me to do similar work for them. This contract will enable me to create a portfolio of interviews. I also told Trédaniel that I would give them the interviews I had previously done with a number of their authors, such as Don Miguel Ruiz.

What an amazing abundant manifestation. I am being paid to do what I love best! I am so excited and I feel so empowered. On so many levels, this opportunity is going to create more abundance. It is going to be a win-win situation for everyone involved. I'm very grateful for that, and I will be happy to have my book published with them too.

WE EACH HAVE OUR PATH

What has worked for me, may not work for you. We each have our unique path. The whole idea of this book is to share my experiences with you and possibly help you discover a path of your own. There is a flow to life that you create with your own expectations, your own doubts, and everything else that comes up along the way. No matter what happens, it is important to always love and nurture who you are and remember that your life is a journey. It's not just one thing, but a series of things. My being able to do what I am doing now comes as a result of my deciding to make a living from my dreams. In truth, for the past three years, I have been preparing for this moment, and I finally knew that the time had come to take inspired action.

YOUR LIFE IS IN YOUR HANDS

I really wasn't ready to step up to this dream until I realized that I deserved to pursue it, that I had the skills to do what needed to be done, and that so many other important elements had finally aligned. So I just want to remind you that you have your life in your hands. You have choices to make, and you are the person most responsible for what happens. Once you understand that simple truth, life can be so amazing. Every day let's be grateful for the small things that unfold and not get lost in demanding that bigger and better things unfold. Let's allow life to happen and relax into it.

I BELIEVE IN YOU

A magnificent and beautifully abundant adventure is unfolding in my life, and it is so important for me to be able to share it with you. I want to tell you how much I love you and believe in you. Some of you may read that line and think, *"How can she believe in me? She doesn't even know me."* But the truth is that I do know you because I am you and you are me. We share the same energy field and the same planet. We have gone through many of the same heartbreaking experiences. Some of those experiences have even shut down our hearts for a time and driven us to fear that they had destroyed us. But we survived, and we are *still here* to develop our full potential to live our best lives. This is the time to build our confidence, to give ourselves love, and to live our unique passions. This is the time to be true to ourselves instead of trying to be somebody else.

TIME TO HEAL NOW

I feel quite chatty today. I feel like opening up. I'm going to take this opportunity to share what I'm thinking and feeling right now with you.

I have this recurring thought about the gratitude I feel for living at my mother's house. After having lost my job, I had no other option but to live back at home. It was humiliating at age 32 not to be out on my own, but at the same time, it turned out to be a beautiful thing. Life brought me to live with my mom and do some important soul work. As a result, I think we have become closer since last summer than we've ever been in our lives, and I'm very grateful for that.

Now, as I gain financial independence through the contract I have negotiated, I've been thinking that I would like to live near the beach. I feel very blessed to be able to heal these aspects of myself while my parents are still alive and before having made a life commitment to a boyfriend, a husband, and maybe even children of my own.

DANCE OF LIFE

I allow myself to take some risks. Either they pay off or they don't; and if they don't, something else always opens up. It is just like a dance, one step at a time, going with the flow, being present to the energy. There is magic in the dance of life. It is about co-creating together, taking inspired action, embracing life, and confidently moving forward in trust. The more confident you become, the more magical the dance can be. I look forward to opening my heart even further and discovering even more magic.

I also find it inspiring to be in nature. I often talk to trees. I always remember my interview with Satish Kumar, such a beautiful human being, when we talked about the importance of communicating with nature. I have done so much self healing in this way. Trees have a very calming effect on me. When I put my hand on a tree or give one of them a big hug, I often repeat to myself, *"I am. I am."* I feel a powerful connection and a sense of oneness with trees. This may seem a strange concept to some, but I not only see the beauty of trees, I also feel the power of their wisdom. We should respect nature because it is part of us and we are part of it.

I am smiling right now as I walk along a beautiful little river in the forest not far from where my mom lives. It is like going through a mind and body detox. Right now, I am thinking about my old behaviors, my old patterns, and my old ways of doing things.

GUIDANCE FROM WITHIN

In my first book, I was at a place in my life where I felt so lost and needed guidance, so I went in search of it by asking other people for advice. In my life now, I ask for outside advice less often, because I have come to trust my own inner guidance to move me in the direction I need to go. My wish is that you will also follow your true calling and live a life of abundance, because that is your birthright. In childhood, we often let opportunities pass us by because we didn't take the time to look at the situation with nurturing and loving eyes. We were hard on ourselves because we didn't know how to fully appreciate our experiences. Our parents did their best, but they were sharing thoughts and behaviors with us based on the teachings of their own parents. So now, it is about healing all of that. It is about giving ourselves the love that we've been seeking on the outside by looking on the inside and understanding that the love we most need has been there all along.

ABUNDANCE FOR ALL!

So, my beautiful co-creator, as abundance is beginning to enter my life, I am coming to the end of this book. The thing to remember is that this world is filled with abundance. There is a place for all of us. I'm opening myself to greater abundance and more creativity. I am stepping up the quality of my work and giving more of my heart to everything I do. There is no such thing as competition. We each have our own calling and a unique way of doing things. What we have learned through our experiences, and what we have been protective of in the past—whether it was thoughts, ideas, or the best way of doing things—is the exact sort of information that we should be sharing with others. Possibly because I was an only child, I am late to understanding this. But now that I do, I am healing that part of myself by opening up more and more. It is through the act of helping others that we grow most of all.

March 21st

WONDERFUL AS IT IS RIGHT NOW

I'm doing a walk in nature. I just stopped by the river and looking at it realized that I already have everything I need right now. I wanted to live near water, and here is the river. I wanted to be near nature, and here are the woods. I wanted to be in an amazing relationship, and I have wonderful friends all around the world. I have good family communication. I am healthy. I'm eating nourishing, vibrant foods. I have a roof over my head. I have a good relationship with my mother and dad and other members of my family.

I have a wonderful network of supportive friends. When I travel, I am always welcome to stay at their homes. I'm interviewing amazing top authors around the world. I have a wonderful camera that enables me to film beautiful moments and share them with the world. I have the time to record my life experiences as they unfold and share them with you. So really, what more is there to ask for? Life is wonderful just as it is right now. Thank you. Thank you. Thank you.

FREE AND GROUNDED

By the end of my first book, I felt like I had reached the mountain top and that I was finally free. Now, I am still free, but I am also grounded by life on earth and nature in its purest form. It's good to be grounded. It feels wonderful. It combines the feeling of freedom with a sense of centeredness and peacefulness. It is the perfect balance of earthly and cosmic values. It is the two forces coming together and bringing light into the essence of who I am. It is an undefinable thing, but I am living the truth of it fully. As each day passes, I am becoming more of myself.

I am grateful for all the blessings in my life. I am grateful to be living in this lifetime. I am grateful for all the moments of communion and union, of success and gratitude, of comfort and love, and for abundance in all its forms. It's here. It's everywhere. It is all around us all the time. It's like love. It's like air. We're breathing it. I'm it. You're it. Collectively, we are all the definition of it. There is a natural flow. Yes, we go in and out of that flow, but that's okay. All we need to do is relax and jump back in the flow again.

ABUNDANCE IS EVERYWHERE

Abundance is here right now. It is all around us. Look around! Go into nature and you'll see it everywhere. It is here on these pages. It is here in how your heart feels when you read these pages. It is here when you look into a baby's eyes. It is here when you take a deep, refreshing breath and fill your lungs. It is here when you smile. It is here when you look into a mirror at your own image and realize that, in seeing yourself, you are seeing the miracle, the essence, and the spark of life. This is the vibration. This is the eternal dimension of your being.

LIVING A JUICY LIFE

If we live our lives as spiritual beings having a human experience, it changes everything. It makes it so much more exciting to be alive. At times, things can feel somewhat bizarre and surreal, but at the same time, life-giving and astonishing. It is like seeing the miracle of life around you in all its forms; because life does have a form, a structure, and a density. So if we see ourselves as physical, we are this little bitty thing having one experience on one planet. But when we see ourselves as spiritual, we come to understand that we are limitless; then life gets juicy.

The more we remember that we are spiritual beings who are part of a vast Universe and that we each have a role and a mission here, the easier it is to be grateful for our time on Earth. In all of its contrasting forms, life is beautiful. By opening ourselves up and going with the flow, life happens, and it will show us the way. You can let go of fear because you will be protected and guided. Once you open yourself up to that guidance, you will understand that you have chosen to be here in order to live something, to do something, and to be a part of something incredible. The World is in the process of change right now, a huge change, and you are here to bear witness and participate in that shift.

SUPPORTED BY THE UNIVERSE

I realize that the relationship I have with money still needs healing and nurturing. I am creating a balanced, harmonious life filled with abundance on every level. I am attracting and manifesting joy, warmth, friendship, wonderful adventures, knowledge, wisdom, international discoveries, and limitless inspiration. I'm grateful for this journey and for having the chance to see life from this new, delightful, and unlimited vantage point. Thank you. Thank you. Thank you.

April 1st

I am grateful for the time when I had no money because the experiences I went through taught me so many valuable lessons. I learned that, while it feels good to have money, it doesn't define who I am. I now understand that the Universe brought about my job loss to see what is real, to re-open my heart, to heal, and to open to the real beauty and abundance of life. Now, thanks to all the steps I took on that path, I am making a beautiful living doing what I most love and what I'm meant to do. This feels so right and so good in my heart. I am in the flow, and I am lovingly supported by the Universe every step of the way.

We come from different backgrounds with different families and different educations, but we all come from the same Source. We're all spirit. We're all limitless. We create our reality. It starts inside. It is about knowing who we are on a deeper level. It is about vibrational abundance; the real abundance, the unlimited access that we all have to everything in the world. Outside things do not represent who we are. Being truly abundant is in knowing that you are pure love, pure energy, and that everything in your life is working out perfectly just as it is. So relax, and move with confidence toward the next adventure with an open heart.

TO BE CONTINUED…

AFTERWORD

There is something I want to say to each of you personally. Claim what you want in this life. Claim what you really, really want. Claim your heart's desire, and don't feel any guilt about doing so. You deserve it, co-creator. Spread your wings!!

Just think about how much genuine love, effort, and—at times—even unconditional love you have given to others in your life. You have generously given so very much, and it is natural law that what you have given will come back to you. You must now allow it, step back, and let it come in unconditionally.

Ask for magical moments, people with an open heart, answers, compassion, forgiveness, authenticity, and assistance, and watch what happens. Watch, listen, and open your eyes, and you will begin to see how much support you truly have from the Universe on your journey of the heart.

Have faith and trust. The time is now.

If you feel like reaching me, you can email me at lilou@liloumace. com. You can also post a message on my Facebook page at www.facebook.com/liloumacewebTV.

I send you much, much love.

Lilou

ACKNOWLEDGEMENTS

I want to thank all of the wonderful co-creators around the world who have been supporting me. Our community has grown into millions of connections and video views because of our efforts. We have created this inspiring archive of knowledge and have brought people together. I am proud of our work! This planet is a better place because of it. I am so grateful for all of the love, the comments, the support all along...and your loyalty. I feel so blessed. Thank you.

I am grateful for all the wonderful 100-Day Reality Challenge community members who have been participating so actively around the world in transforming each others' reality, season after season, to one that is aligned with our true Self. It is so much fun and juicy to have you side by side on this journey. I am especially grateful for Mascha, Clarissa, Mari, Megan, Antonio, Laura, Karen, Chris, Sandy, Bryan, Lisa, Jessica, Terry, Kim, Sue, Steffani, Annina, Lynn, David, Carol, Kristi, Justen, Liv, Lili, Sherri, Katy, Lena, Tamara, Amber, Nicole, Mark, Dawn, Helena, Julie, Elizabeth, Kevin, Paris, Veronika, Martta, Nathalie, Donna, Marianne, and Doug. You guys are my rock.

I want to thank my wonderful parents, Irene Martin and Jean-Yves. My soul will be eternally grateful for all the wonderful life lessons I received from you. I love you deeply.

Finally, I want to acknowledge three special people who have made this book a reality. My Dutch friend, Baptist de Pape, who has been an amazing, supportive friend all along, as you discovered in this book. Linda, who edited this book to be what it is now. Wow! Great work, co-creator...this is our baby!! LOL. And finally, Lynda Mangoro, the wonderful multi-talented friend and co-worker who supports many of the wonderful juicy projects I get into. Lynda, you bring the spark. I love you.

Last, but not least, I want to thank *you* for embarking with me on this journey. You were in my thoughts as I wrote this book. You gave me strength in the hardest moments, during panic attacks, and when I had lack of faith and fears arised on this journey to an open heart. YES, you were there. I felt your presence and talked to you, my beautiful co-creator, all along. You picking up this book confirms it.

Thank you from the bottom of my heart.

ABOUT THE AUTHOR

Lilou Macé was born in Santa Barbara, California to French parents who were restaurateurs. She spent most of her youth growing up in Nantes, France.

Lilou is an entrepreneur, inspirational author, and web sensation. Her first venture was starting her own internet marketing company. Since then, she has gone on to write books, start her own publishing company, travel the globe interviewing *New York Times* bestselling authors, and meet some really inspiring people along the way.

Lilou is also the co-founder of an online community called "Co-Creating Our Reality: 100-Day Reality Challenge." As of 2011, the community has 7000+ members in 140 countries worldwide. Initially inspired by Oprah, Lilou began producing her own inspirational TV show in November of 2006. Originally called *My Juicy Life,* and later titled *Live a Juicy Life*, the show follows Lilou as she interviews the authors of motivational, spiritual, and self-help books; a practice she still continues on her YouTube channel. (www.youtube.com/liloumace)

As of September 2011, Lilou has over 10 million viewers on YouTube, has conducted 700+ interviews, and is one of the fastest-growing Web TV hosts globally. Her videos are translated into many languages for viewers around the globe. Her vision is to develop and expand Web TV programs in all the main languages and countries around the world.

Lilou's mission is to create and host an international communication network to "inspire, motivate, and empower millions of people to pursue their dreams" and to "help spread joy, freedom, and personal awakening."

As of this printing, Lilou resides "on the road," as she is currently travelling and interviewing authors and spiritual teachers for the Juicy Living Tour. To learn more about the tour, and to check out interviews with some of the world's most inspiring people, go to www.JuicyLivingTour.com.

For Lilou's latest updates, visit her website (www.liloumace. com) or log on to Facebook and catch up with her there (www. Facebook.com/LiloumacewebTV).

ABOUT THE TEAM

LINDA PAPCIAK

Linda is a lifelong writer, dreamer and truth-seeker. She attended the University of Illinois with a focus on Journalism. She has worked as a copywriter in both broadcast and print advertising. She has also served as an executive assistant in many related fields including advertising, marketing and public relations. Linda realized one of her "big dreams" through her collaboration with Lilou Macé as copyeditor on *I Had No Money and I Liked It*. Through Linda's professional writing and editing skills, she hopes to help others live their "big dreams" too. Linda resides in Chicago, Illinois. She can be reached at: Soulecho29@aol.com

"My first introduction to Lilou Macé came in 2009 when I happened upon one of her YouTube videos. I was instantly taken with this young French woman's openness, curiosity and thirst for spiritual knowledge. Countless videos later and after reading her book, I *Lost My Job and I Liked It*, I knew that Lilou's tireless efforts to pursue her own dreams and share her journey with the world, had re-awakened the dreamer inside of me, too. Working with Lilou on *I Had No Money and I Liked It* was a true labor of love. This second installment of her candid and incredibly inspiring story moved me deeply as I know it will you."

LYNDA MANGORO

Lynda is an artist and author. She has a degree in Multimedia Systems and has experience working as a web developer for a top London company. Lynda has recently realised her dream of working independently and offers a range of services utilising her artistic, graphic, and technical skills in order to help people share their own gifts with the world. This has included creating the logo and website for Lilou's *Juicy Living Tour.* Lynda has also written a novel for teens, *Awakening of the Dream Riders*, a metaphysical fantasy which is more a work of soul truth than fiction, and an illustrated book for younger children, *Where's the Magic Wand?,* which is first in a series of memorable and whimsical rhyming stories which convey important and powerful messages for children. Both of these titles are being published by Lilou Mace's publishing company; *Juicy Living Publishing*. Lynda lives in West Sussex with her husband Michael and their three cherished sons. Visit www.LyndaMangoro.com and www.facebook.com/ LyndaMangoroCreations. Contact lynda at lynda@mangoro. co.uk.

"I came across Lilou's videos in 2010, at a time when I was taking a big leap in my own journey of self discovery. I was immediately drawn to the strength with which this amazing lady was following her dreams and trusting her heart, whilst being very open about her fears. Synchronously, through one of her videos, I discovered Lilou was seeking an artist to create a character logo for her *Juicy Living Tour*. I emailed immediately, buzzing with excitement and it was the start of a beautiful co-creational relationship and a much cherished friendship. The last year has simply been a dream come true and my greatest wish is to continue following my intuition, trusting it will continue to lead me along my soul path and contribute to the big shift that is happening right now. With inspirational people like Lilou in the world – it's easy to believe in the clear vision of heaven on Earth that we are awakening to."

SARAH CISCO

Sarah is a freelance editor and intuitive healer living in Indianapolis. She got her start in publishing working as an editor for a couple of large technical publishers. She has since branched out on her own to take on more exciting projects. Working on meaningful books that inspire people is her priority. Sarah loves organic food, yoga, meditation, pugs, and Dave Chappelle (for turning down $50 million dollars for the right reasons).

ANNE-SOPHIE JESSEL

Anne-Sophie has always been an artist at heart. She captured Lilou's juiciness in a photograph that was selected for the book's cover. Having spent some of her career as a consultant, Anne-Sophie now expresses her creativity through drawing, painting, fashion, and photography. Her vision is to one day have a "Maison du Bonheur" in France—an artistic and well-being retreat center.

Synchronicities brought Lilou and Anne-Sophie together in London in 2009, and they have been great friends ever since. Their friendship had a monumental impact on Lilou's opening of the heart, as described in this book. Anne-Sophie is now involved in various aspects of the Juicy Living Tour and with Lilou's webTVs worldwide. annesophiejessel@gmail.com

I LOST MY JOB AND I LIKED IT
BY LILOU MACE

In this book, the prequel to *I Had No Money and I Liked It*, international internet guru Lilou 'The Big L' Mace believes in the Law of Attraction (as revealed in The Secret) and that we can create anything we want using the power of our thoughts. Drawn to the USA from France, she used this law to co-found the '100-Day Reality Challenge' community, to build a following of thousands of YouTubers, and to 'manifest' a meeting with Oprah Winfrey, someone she greatly admires without wishing to copy. ('The Big L' believes that being true to your unique Self is crucial to success.)

Now she's in London and she's lost her job. The time has come to test her beliefs to the limit: at a time of global crisis can she use the Law of Attraction to find her dream job, and thereby 'empower millions' to do likewise?

This is her stream-of-consciousness diary, written over a month, from the moment she was sacked. Travel with her as she grapples with doubt, relishes avocados and finds something good, even in what at first appear to be the most disheartening of setbacks. Deploying a battery of mood-shifting, life-enhancing, and possibly reality-changing techniques, she attempts to prove to herself – and to you! – that a better way of living is possible. … That one can live a truly Juicy Life!

While 30-something Lilou would probably get on with the fictional Bridget Jones, her real-life diary is a very different thing. Humble, moving, funny and perceptive, it epitomises the style of leadership she believes the world desperately needs. If Lilou's approach works, this book might just be The Survival Guide for Our Times, and she the vanguard of a revolution.

Read it, and, most importantly, try it out!

ISBN 978-0-9562546-0-3

"Lilou Mace is a fountain of energy and confidence, yet when she lost her highly paid job she suffered, as all of us can, from a momentary blow to her self confidence. This book is her journal of her thoughts and actions as she discovers, in fact, that her life has just been set free so she can do what she really feels to be authentic. For anyone who is looking to use the Law of Attraction and to change their life this will be a most useful book.
– Dr Allan Hunter – Author of *Stories We Need to Know* and *The Six Archetypes of Love*

 *Juicy Living* Publishing

Juicy Living Publishing was founded by Lilou Macé in 2009 when she published her first book, *I Lost My Job and I Liked It*. In 2011, Lilou went on to launch her Juicy Living Tour, traveling around the world interviewing juicy people, including many renowned authors and teachers, bringing information and inspiration to millions via her Web TV channel. Following her inner guidance system, in early 2011 Lilou was inspired to open her publishing company up to other authors, with the intention of contributing to the global conversation of empowerment and awakening consciousness.

With the inevitable expansion of thoughts and practices that relate to spiritual ideals and internal development during this recognized time of shifting energies, Juicy Living Publishing aims to give authors the opportunity to share their messages and teachings with as wide an audience as possible. Our vision is to produce resources that promote a juicy way of living for all our readers. Worldwide.

Juicy Living Publishing is committed to producing books of high quality and high value to its readers of all ages; children, teens, and adults. We welcome submissions from both published and new authors. Please see our submissions page for guideline at www.JuicyLivingPublishing.com.

ALSO FROM JUICY LIVING PUBLISHING

I LOST MY JOB AND I LIKED IT BY LILOU MACE

This book is the prequel to *I Had No Money and I Liked It*. Lilou has lost her job. The time has come to test her beliefs to the limit: at a time of global crisis can she use the Law of Attraction to find her dream job, and thereby 'empower millions' to do likewise? This is her 30-day stream-of-consciousness diary, from the moment she was lost her job. Travel with her as she grapples with doubt, relishes avocados and finds something to be grateful for in each and every step of her job search.

ISBN: 978-0-9562546-0-3

AWAKENING OF THE DREAM RIDERS BY LYNDA MANGORO

Kyra Sutton likes to think of herself as an ordinary fourteen year old girl. Until she makes an extraordinary discovery… She's a Dream Rider, and she's not the only one. This new found ability plunges Kyra and her friends into adventures to realms they couldn't have imagined in their wildest dreams. Along the way deep truths about themselves and the world around them begin to unfold, and the group gradually awaken to their true purpose in life. Nothing will ever be ordinary again…

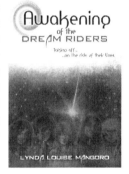

ISBN 978-0-9562546-2-7

WHERE'S THE MAGIC WAND? BY LYNDA MANGORO

As well as being a memorable and whimsical rhyming story, rich with vibrant illustrations, this tale conveys an important and powerful message for young children – that we all create our realities and shape our lives through our thoughts and beliefs. What better gift to give them than this powerful knowledge?

ISBN 978-0-9562546-1-0

MESSAGES FROM CO-CREATORS

I am holding your first book in my hands and I can't wait to get started. I loved a snippet I glanced at about why kids should travel... I was sent to Spain by my parents when I was nine to see the world. They didn't know that it would mean I would catch the travelling bug. Now I live in another country then them... LOL. From Paris to Bristol... England is now my home.

- **Anges de Lumiere**

You gave me courage to say today I bless my homelessness. I feel free and love the excitement of blessing everything. Changes are wonderful once we get on the wave to ride then the fear is found to be nothing. Ive been more stressed for NO reason So why worry as LONG as we get up and suit up and show up for our life its all good. Yes Yes Yes.

- **Cindy Schreiber**

Lilou Mace has been such a great inspiration in my life and continues to be so daily. I see her really living the dream, manifesting the life she desires and that, to me, is the greatest inspiration of all and encourages me to follow my dreams.

- **Jean Dayton Artist**

I journeyed from my African home with you Lilou Mace, I opened my eyes, and my heart, along the way I learnt from the people who opened their hearts to you, and became a privileged member of a select group of "Lilou lovers". I am forever grateful for taking me on this heart journey, my spirit has changed. I'm a better person because of you!

- **Wendy Spivey**

I am so glad to have discovered Lilou. She is an example of following one's heart, trusting in the universe, and living a juicy life. Many times I have watched an interview that has challenged me to live with an open heart and an open mind. She has reminded me on several occasions to have a little faith. I am so grateful to follow Lilou's journey. Her journey has strengthened mine. We are all in this together. It is so awesome when juicy energies from all walks of life converge. Thank you Lilou from one beautiful co-creator to another.

- Kim Piche-Guthoerl

Lilou is the living embodiment of inspiration! Not only does she follow her divine inner voice, but sharing the journey with so many others as she goes, teaching her learning process with great masters, and laughing in the face of insecurity as she takes life by the reigns and creates a literal community of the most evolved beings, the process of her own evolution has become an incredible tool of it's own for the upliftment of all humanity. I am so grateful to have her in my life.

- Crystal Hutchens

Lilou you are passion and authenticity personified...you have taken us all on this journey with you...and we are soo blessed by YOU and your precious heart.

- Gaia Subren

Lilou Macé has made the jump into the unknown, in search of herself and 'truth', with the bold mission and act of love of bringing to as many people possible the many and varied wonders of having faith in the joyous spiritual life.

- Mark Lummis

Lilou Mace has dived head first into her dreams and has made it her mission to take us with her. Touring the globe like a synchronistic gypsy shaman with no money and no job yet strangely sharing the secrets to making our dreams come true. Unrealistic? You have no idea. Her journey is truly "Unreal" and the best part is she shows us how it's done.

- Louis Hansell

Wow Lilou! I've received your eBook "I Lost My Job And I Liked It" as a present two years ago, and I started reading it. And then I put it down. I could not hear the words entirely, because the timing was not right yet. Two weeks ago I felt drawn to open and read the eBook again, and it feels like a flight-beacon to me. I hear the words loud and clear, I let them in. I feel the frequency of my dream job, I feel how it feels like, and I am very close to things unfolding themselves. Your book is a travel companion. An invitation to do what I love. To go all the way. To continue to dream big, and accept living a big life. Lilou, you are amazing in your quest to be the best you can be, and inspiring others to be the best they can be. You teach by example. What makes you radiant is your uniqueness and appreciation for yourself and others. Being just who you are, also sharing your challenges with the rest of the world. This makes you brave. Thank you for being a living example. It is nice to have a beautiful deliberate, loving co-creator among us, reminding us of our own creative brilliance.

- Eliane Haseth

Lilou, your enthusiasm is infectious! I needed a power pick-me-up and your interviews always do it for me! Thank you. I don't know how you find some of your subjects but I ALWAYS learn something and expand my thought process when I watch your interviews. Thank you Lilou. Your vision to "inspire, motivate and empower millions of people to pursue their dreams" and to "help spread joy, freedom and personal awakening" is working. You ARE helping millions. I am happy to be included in that group, you have really helped me. Knowledge is power, your interviews are spreading knowledge to the world…your subjects are fascinating. You ask interesting questions…you are empowering the planet.

- Stan Ketcik

I just wanted to let you know that I love your work and think that your purpose and mission is going to be a pivotal ingredient for shifting the planet. Your interviews amaze me and I know that this is only going to get bigger for you and the whole planet. Thanks for your commitment to taking us into the future and allowing humanity to live the life that we were always meant to.

- David Reid